SPELLING MADE EASY

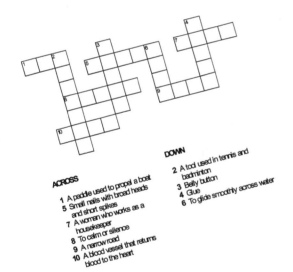

ACROSS

1 A paddle used to propel a boat
5 Small nails with broad heads and short spikes
7 A woman who works as a housekeeper
8 To calm or silence
9 A narrow road
10 A blood vessel that returns blood to the heart

DOWN

2 A tool used in tennis and badminton
3 Belly button
4 Glue
6 To glide smoothly across water

```
E H C A C L B T
 N E E D I D O T
 N K P A A L K F
C L H Z L D B E
T B E A Z A N I
 I C A W Q E J N
A V X L E N K T
G R N H E K N W
```

CONNIE SCHENKELBERG

© 2010 by Connie Schenkelberg / Everyday Education, LLC

Made Easy Books™
A Division of
Everyday Education
Making Time for Things That Matter
P.O. Box 549
Ashland, VA 23005
www.Everyday-Education.com
www.Spelling-Made-Easy.com

Schenkelberg, Connie

Spelling made easy: The homonym way to better spelling/ Connie Schenkelberg

ISBN: 978-0-9774685-2-2

1. Education—Home Schooling. 2. Education—Reference. 3. Reference—Handbooks & Manuals. I. Title.

The integrity of the upright shall guide them...
Proverbs 11:3a

SPELLING MADE EASY

Background:

For over 30 years, I taught English in a variety of settings. I worked in private and public schools. I home schooled my own children in the upper grades and served as a co-op teacher for a home school group. As an English teacher, I was expected to teach literature, writing, research skills, grammar, and spelling.

My degree in secondary education taught me how to teach literature and writing. Research skills I learned in high school and refined in college. But grammar and spelling didn't really fit into the college curriculum. By that, I mean most teacher training schools show students how to teach just about everything *except* grammar and spelling. So, what do teachers do? Many just ignore these subjects.

Well, that won't do. Thus began a search for effective spelling instruction.

Teaching Spelling:

I found two good approaches. First, to lay a great foundation for spelling, Romalda Spalding's *The Writing Road to Reading* is a great way to go. Recommended for students in grades K-6, this system uses a multisensory approach to develop the letter-sound connection (phonics) and then expand it into reading and spelling.

The second is homonyms. Most of us have word processing programs that catch true spelling errors. However, these programs cannot alert the writer to homonym errors. Thus, it makes sense to me to study homonyms. **And**, this is what is tested on middle school standardized tests.

I used homonyms as the basis of my spelling instruction the last few years I was the classroom. My students had the *highest scores* in our building, and their spelling errors in written assignments went down dramatically.

Suggested Use:

Spelling Made Easy is intended to make spelling instruction easy and painless. There are 290 homonym groups in the book. Every 10 groups form a lesson, which includes the list with their definitions plus **4 puzzles**.

This book can be used for one or two years of instruction. To help you, I have placed suggested assignments following every lesson page. They're suggestions only, but they may make your life a little easier.

Thank you for choosing *Spelling Made Easy*. I hope it serves you and your students well.

Connie Schenkelberg

TABLE OF CONTENTS

LESSON 1: HOMONYMS 1 – 10

1.	A lot: Allot: Alot:	Many. To set aside for someone's use. NEVER, EVER correct
2.	Bail: Bale:	Money deposited with the courts to assure that a defendant will appear in court. A large mound of hay packaged for animal consumption.
3.	Cache: Cash:	A place to hide valuables. Money.
4.	Dawn: Don:	Early morning, just as the sun is rising. Old term meaning to put on (as in clothes)
5.	Ewe: You:	A female sheep. Second person pronoun (not *me* or *he/she/it*).
6.	Faint: Feint:	Pale, weak. Soft or quiet. Dizzy, woozy. A trick or maneuver.
7.	Gait: Gate:	Walk, pace. The opening in a fence.
8.	Hail: Hale:	To call out a greeting. Frozen rain. Healthy.
9.	Idle: Idol:	Lazy; not working. An object that is worshiped.
10.	Knead: Kneed: Need:	To manipulate bread dough so it will rise. To use the knee, past tense. Something that is necessary.

Assignment Schedule for One-Year Course

Monday:	Give students the list above. Have them copy Groups 1-3 into their spelling notebook. The reason for this is to help students remember what they're studying. The acts of writing and thinking about the words and their differences help students retain the information longer.
Tuesday:	Have students copy Groups 4-6 into their spelling notebook. Do Puzzle 1.
Wednesday:	Have students copy Groups 7-8 into their spelling notebook. Do Puzzle 2.
Thursday:	Have students copy Groups 9-10 into their spelling notebook. Do Puzzle 3.
Friday:	Do Puzzle 4 – without the lesson sheet or spelling notebook.
Friday fun:	Using as many of these homonyms as possible, write a paragraph about yourself.

Assignment Schedule for Two-Year Course

Monday:	Give students the list above. Have them copy Groups 1-2 into their spelling notebook. The reason for this is to help students remember what they're studying. The acts of writing and thinking about the words and their differences help students retain the information longer.
Tuesday:	Have students copy Groups 3-4 into their spelling notebook.
Wednesday:	Have students copy Groups 5-6 into their spelling notebook.
Thursday:	Have students copy Groups 7-8 into their spelling notebook.
Friday:	Have students copy Groups 9-10 into their spelling notebook.
Monday:	Do Puzzle 1.
Tuesday:	Do Puzzle 2.
Wednesday:	Do Puzzle 3.
Thursday:	Do Puzzle 4. – without the lesson sheet or spelling notebook.
Friday fun:	Using as many of these homonyms as possible, write a paragraph about yourself.

HOMONYMS 1-10, PUZZLE 1

Use the clues to find the answers in the crossword puzzle.

ACROSS

- **4** healthy
- **5** money
- **8** pale, weak; soft or quiet; dizzy, woozy
- **9** a place to hide valuables
- **10** lazy; not working
- **11** an object that is worshiped
- **12** NEVER, EVER correct
- **14** walk, pace
- **15** to manipulate bread dough so it will rise
- **17** something that is necessary

DOWN

- **1** a female sheep
- **2** early morning, just as the sun is rising
- **3** the opening in a fence
- **6** to call out a greeting; frozen rain
- **7** money deposited with the courts to assure that a defendant will appear in court
- **8** a trick or maneuver
- **12** to set aside for someone's use
- **13** a large mound of hay packaged for animal consumption
- **15** to use the knee, past tense
- **16** old term meaning to put on (as in clothes)

HOMONYMS 1-10, PUZZLE 2

Use the clues to find the answers in the word search puzzle. Words can be found horizontally, vertically, or diagonally.

```
B   K   N   E   A   D   M   N   F   M   F
K   N   W   A   D   N   E   L   A   H   M
B   N   L   E   J   F   B   A   I   L   T
T   A   E   W   Y   C   N   X   N   O   L
N   C   L   E   L   T   E   O   L   O   G
I   A   N   E   D   O   Z   L   D   Z   A
E   C   G   L   B   L   A   I   D   C   T
F   H   C   A   R   A   H   D   A   I   E
Q   E   U   M   I   A   N   S   E   J   X
M   O   D   M   I   T   H   C   N   E   T
Y   M   Z   L   Z   F   A   I   N   T   N
```

_____ 1. money
_____ 2. a female sheep
_____ 3. healthy
_____ 4. to set aside for someone's use
_____ 5. walk, pace
_____ 6. a trick or maneuver
_____ 7. to use the knee, past tense
_____ 8. old term meaning to put on (as in clothes)
_____ 9. NEVER, EVER correct
_____ 10. a place to hide valuables
_____ 11. early morning, just as the sun is rising
_____ 12. second person pronoun (not _me_ or _he/she/it_)
_____ 13. something that is necessary
_____ 14. pale, weak; soft or quiet; dizzy, woozy
_____ 15. the opening in a fence
_____ 16. to call out a greeting; frozen rain
_____ 17. an object that is worshiped
_____ 18. to manipulate bread dough so it will rise
_____ 19. lazy; not working
_____ 20. a large mound of hay packaged for animal consumption
_____ 21. money deposited to ensure a defendant will appear in court

10   Made with 1-2-3 Word Search Maker

HOMONYMS 1-10, PUZZLE 3

Use the clues to find the answers in the crossword puzzle.

ACROSS

4 healthy
6 NEVER, EVER correct
7 a trick or maneuver
13 old term meaning to put on (as in clothes)
14 to set aside for someone's use
15 the opening in a fence
16 money deposited with the courts to assure that a defendant will appear in court
18 a place to hide valuables
19 to use the knee, past tense

DOWN

1 money
2 walk, pace
3 second person pronoun (not me or he/she/it)
5 a female sheep
7 pale, weak, soft or quiet; dizzy, woozy
8 something that is necessary
9 an object that is worshiped
10 to manipulate bread dough so it will rise
11 lazy; not working
12 to call out a greeting; frozen rain
16 a large mound of hay packaged for animal consumption
17 early morning, just as the sun is rising

HOMONYMS 1-10, PUZZLE 4

Use the clues to find the answers in the word search puzzle. Words can be found horizontally, vertically, or diagonally.

```
M  F  H  R  F  Z  J  M  X  W  L  J
K  N  E  A  D  H  B  A  I  L  T  N
N  K  R  I  N  M  T  L  O  K  H  E
E  F  R  C  N  O  K  D  U  G  N  E
T  L  A  B  L  T  I  O  C  A  M  D
R  S  A  L  A  N  Y  T  A  I  Q  V
H  P  A  H  N  L  O  Y  C  T  J  Y
K  Y  N  W  A  D  E  D  H  Z  G  T
E  N  B  N  Z  H  N  N  E  A  E  O
L  R  E  F  A  I  N  T  T  Q  W  L
D  P  L  E  N  X  R  E  L  M  E  A
I  Z  K  T  D  C  L  I  A  H  B  D
```

_____ 1. lazy; not working
_____ 2. money
_____ 3. a female sheep
_____ 4. an object that is worshiped
_____ 5. healthy
_____ 6. a trick or maneuver
_____ 7. to use the knee, past tense
_____ 8. the opening in a fence
_____ 9. old term meaning to put on (as in clothes)
_____ 10. NEVER, EVER correct
_____ 11. a place to hide valuables
_____ 12. early morning, just as the sun is rising
_____ 13. to set aside for someone's use
_____ 14. walk, pace
_____ 15. something that is necessary
_____ 16. pale, weak; soft or quiet; dizzy, woozy
_____ 17. to call out a greeting; frozen rain
_____ 18. to manipulate bread dough so it will rise
_____ 19. second person pronoun (not *me* or *he/she/it*)
_____ 20. a large mound of hay packaged for animal consumption
_____ 21. money deposited to ensure a defendant will appear in court

LESSON 2: HOMONYMS 11 – 20

11.	Lain: Lane:	To lie in a resting position. A narrow road.
12.	Made: Maid:	To make, past tense. A woman who works as a housekeeper.
13.	Naval: Navel:	Relating to the navy. Belly button.
14.	Oar: Or: Ore:	A paddle used to propel a boat. A conjunction indicating a choice between 2 things. Raw mineral dug out of the earth.
15.	Paced: Paste:	To walk back and forth, past tense. Glue.
16.	Quiet: Quite:	To calm or to silence. Enough. *Near homonym.*
17.	Rack: Wrack:	A framework for holding goods. Something that is ruined.
18.	Sail: Sale:	To glide smoothly across something, typically water. A canvas cloth used on a sailboat. An event in which prices are marked down.
19.	Tacks: Tax:	Small nails with broad heads and short metal spikes. When the government requires a portion of a person's income as a way of financing its (the government's) expenses.
20.	Vain: Vane: Vein:	Conceited or proud. Ineffective or hopeless. A rotating blade. A blood vessel that returns blood to the heart.

Assignment Schedule for One-Year Course

Monday:	Give students the list above. Have them copy Groups 11-13 into their spelling notebook.
Tuesday:	Have students copy Groups 14-16 into their spelling notebook. Do Puzzle 1.
Wednesday:	Have students copy Groups 17-18 into their spelling notebook. Do Puzzle 2.
Thursday:	Have students copy Groups 19-20 into their spelling notebook. Do Puzzle 3.
Friday:	Do Puzzle 4 – without the lesson sheet or spelling notebook.
Friday fun:	Write two rhyming couplets with some of these words.

Assignment Schedule for Two-Year Course

Monday:	Give students the list above. Have them copy Groups 11-12 into their spelling notebook.
Tuesday:	Have students copy Groups 13-14 into their spelling notebook.
Wednesday:	Have students copy Groups 15-16 into their spelling notebook.
Thursday:	Have students copy Groups 17-18 into their spelling notebook.
Friday:	Have students copy Groups 19-20 into their spelling notebook.
Monday:	Do Puzzle 1.
Tuesday:	Do Puzzle 2.
Wednesday:	Do Puzzle 3.
Thursday:	Do Puzzle 4. – without the lesson sheet or spelling notebook.
Friday fun:	Write two rhyming couplets with some of these words.

HOMONYMS 11-20, PUZZLE 1

Use the clues to find the answers in the crossword puzzle.

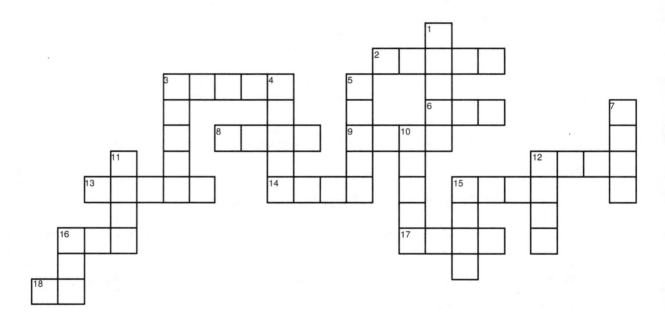

ACROSS

2 something that is ruined
3 to calm or to silence
6 money taken from people to pay government expenses
8 a framework for holding goods
9 a rotating blade
12 conceited or proud; ineffective or hopeless
13 to walk back and forth, past tense
14 to glide smoothly; a canvas cloth used on a sailboat
15 to make, past tense
16 raw mineral dug out of the earth
17 to lie in a resting position
18 a conjunction indicating a choice between 2 things

DOWN

1 glue
3 enough
4 small nails with bread heads and short metal spikes
5 relating to the navy
7 a narrow road
10 belly button
11 an event in which prices are marked down
12 a blood vessel that returns blood to the heart
15 a woman who works as a housekeeper
16 a paddle used to propel a boat

HOMONYMS 11-20, PUZZLE 2

Use the clues to find the answers in the word search puzzle. Words can be found horizontally, vertically, or diagonally.

```
K  C  A  R  W  N  Q  E  N  A  V
C  T  V  X  N  E  Q  U  P  P  E
L  T  M  A  I  G  L  Q  I  N  D
N  B  L  T  A  D  T  A  A  E  R
A  R  A  O  L  M  D  L  S  V  T
V  Q  M  A  D  E  A  T  N  N  R
A  U  Y  R  C  T  A  I  A  Q  R
L  I  L  A  O  C  A  V  D  R  E
J  T  P  I  K  V  E  T  A  C  R
Z  E  H  S  A  L  W  C  D  C  O
P  A  S  T  E  S  K  V  E  I  N
```

_____ 1. glue
_____ 2. enough
_____ 3. belly button
_____ 4. something that is ruined
_____ 5. to lie in a resting position
_____ 6. a rotating blade
_____ 7. to make, past tense
_____ 8. relating to the navy
_____ 9. a paddle used to propel a boat
_____ 10. an event in which prices are marked down
_____ 11. raw mineral dug out of the earth
_____ 12. a narrow road
_____ 13. to walk back and forth, past tense
_____ 14. to calm or to silence
_____ 15. a framework for holding goods
_____ 16. to glide smoothly; a canvas cloth used on a sailboat
_____ 17. a woman who works as a housekeeper
_____ 18. small nails with bread heads and short metal spikes
_____ 19. conceited or proud; ineffective or hopeless
_____ 20. a conjunction indicating a choice between 2 things
_____ 21. a blood vessel that returns blood to the heart
_____ 22. money taken from people to pay government expenses

Made e with 1-2-3 Word Search Maker

HOMONYMS 11-20, PUZZLE 3

Use the clues to find the answers in the crossword puzzle.

ACROSS

1 to make, past tense
3 conceited or proud; ineffective or hopeless
5 to calm or to silence
9 belly button
10 a conjunction indicating a choice between 2 things
11 money taken from people to pay government expenses
12 something that is ruined
13 a narrow road
14 an event in which prices are marked down
16 a rotating blade
17 glue

DOWN

1 a woman who works as a housekeeper
2 to glide smoothly; a canvas cloth used on a sailboat
4 relating to the navy
5 enough
6 small nails with bread heads and short metal spikes
7 a framework for holding goods
8 a paddle used to propel a boat
10 raw mineral dug out of the earth
15 to lie in a resting position
16 a blood vessel that returns blood to the heart
17 to walk back and forth, past tense

Made with Crossword Weaver

HOMONYMS 11-20, PUZZLE 4

Use the clues to find the answers in the word search puzzle. Words can be found horizontally, vertically, or diagonally.

```
T   D   M   A   D   E   L   M   V   N   Q
V   E   B   M   V   A   I   N   D   I   U
K   L   N   K   A   J   F   E   E   A   I
P   A   S   T   E   I   C   M   R   L   T
S   S   V   N   V   A   D   L   O   T   E
X   K   A   T   P   N   N   T   I   T   R
Q   L   C   K   C   A   R   W   Q   A   N
V   U   Y   A   V   V   F   P   C   A   S
E   R   I   R   T   A   H   K   V   N   X
I   J   L   E   O   L   N   E   R   A   O
N   P   J   R   T   Z   L   E   T   Q   Y
```

_____ 1. glue
_____ 2. enough
_____ 3. a narrow road
_____ 4. belly button
_____ 5. a rotating blade
_____ 6. something that is ruined
_____ 7. to make, past tense
_____ 8. relating to the navy
_____ 9. a paddle used to propel a boat
_____ 10. to lie in a resting position
_____ 11. raw mineral dug out of the earth
_____ 12. to walk back and forth, past tense
_____ 13. small nails with bread heads and short metal spikes
_____ 14. a framework for holding goods
_____ 15. to glide smoothly; a canvas cloth used on a sailboat
_____ 16. a woman who works as a housekeeper
_____ 17. conceited or proud; ineffective or hopeless
_____ 18. an event in which prices are marked down
_____ 19. to calm or to silence
_____ 20. a conjunction indicating a choice between 2 things
_____ 21. a blood vessel that returns blood to the heart
_____ 22. money taken from people to pay government expenses

18   Made e with 1-2-3 Word Search Maker

LESSON 3: HOMONYMS 21 – 30

21.	Wade: Weighed:	To walk in shallow water. To check on one's weight, past tense.
22.	Yawn: Yon:	A wide opening of the mouth that occurs when one is sleepy. Old term for "over there."
23.	Accept: Except:	Allow or agree to (match up the "A" with agree). To take away (match up the "ex" with excuse or exit). *Near homonyms.*
24.	Bait: Bate:	Something used to lure something else. To hold back something.
25.	Callous: Callus:	An attitude that is hardened against someone or something. A hardened, thickened area of skin.
26.	Days: Daze:	24-hour periods. Confuse.
27.	Fair: Faire: Fare:	Equitable, even-handed. Also, pale or light colored. A festival, with many things happening at once. The cost of transportation.
28.	Gnu: Knew: New:	Another name for a wildebeest. To know (be aware of), past tense. Something recent; not old.
29.	Hair: Hare:	That which grows on the top of one's head. A rabbit.
30.	In: Inn:	A preposition describing a location. A place that rents rooms to travelers.

Assignment Schedule for One-Year Course

Monday:	Give students the list above. Have them copy Groups 21-23 into their spelling notebook.
Tuesday:	Have students copy Groups 24-26 into their spelling notebook. Do Puzzle 1.
Wednesday:	Have students copy Groups 27-28 into their spelling notebook. Do Puzzle 2.
Thursday:	Have students copy Groups 29-30 into their spelling notebook. Do Puzzle 3.
Friday:	Do Puzzle 4 – without the lesson sheet or spelling notebook.
Friday fun:	Write a paragraph with as many of these homonyms as possible. Writing something fun or whimsical ab out gnus would be interesting.

Assignment Schedule for Two-Year Course

Monday:	Give students the list above. Have them copy Groups 21-22 into their spelling notebook.
Tuesday:	Have students copy Groups 23-24 into their spelling notebook.
Wednesday:	Have students copy Groups 25-26 into their spelling notebook.
Thursday:	Have students copy Groups 27-28 into their spelling notebook.
Friday:	Have students copy Groups 29-30 into their spelling notebook.
Monday:	Do Puzzle 1.
Tuesday:	Do Puzzle 2.
Wednesday:	Do Puzzle 3.
Thursday:	Do Puzzle 4. – without the lesson sheet or spelling notebook.
Friday fun:	Write a paragraph with as many of these homonyms as possible. Writing something fun or whimsical ab out gnus would be interesting.

HOMONYMS 21-30, PUZZLE 1

Use the clues to find the answers in the crossword puzzle.

ACROSS

2 equitable, even-handed. also, pale or light colored
6 something recent; not old
9 the cost of transportation
10 something used to lure something else
11 that which grows on the top of one's head
12 to take away
15 old term for "over there"
16 to walk in shallow water
17 24-hour periods
19 another name for a wildebeest
20 a preposition describing a location
21 to know (be aware of), past tense

DOWN

1 a rabbit
2 a festival, with many things happening at once
3 a place that rents rooms to travelers
4 to hold back something
5 confuse
7 to check on one's weight, past tense
8 an attitude that is hardened against someone or something
13 a hardened, thickened area of skin
14 a wide opening of the mouth that occurs when one is sleepy
18 allow or agree to

HOMONYMS 21-30, PUZZLE 2

Use the clues to find the answers in the word search puzzle. Words can be found horizontally, vertically, or diagonally.

```
T  P  E  C  X  E  L  I  S  A
R  S  S  M  G  E  N  Y  K  C
I  U  K  U  R  N  A  E  N  C
A  L  Y  A  O  D  U  D  E  E
F  L  F  O  W  L  E  A  W  P
Y  A  W  N  N  H  L  W  B  T
R  C  I  N  G  H  E  A  B  N
I  E  R  I  A  F  I  T  C  K
A  Q  E  R  Y  T  M  R  A  B
H  W  E  N  D  A  Z  E  Y  B
```

_____ 1. to walk in shallow water
_____ 2. another name for a wildebeest
_____ 3. confuse
_____ 4. a rabbit
_____ 5. a wide opening of the mouth when one is sleepy
_____ 6. 24-hour periods
_____ 7. something used to lure something else
_____ 8. the cost of transportation
_____ 9. to hold back something
_____ 10. a hardened, thickened area of skin
_____ 11. allow or agree to
_____ 12. old term for "over there"
_____ 13. to check on one's weight, past tense
_____ 14. a festival, with many things happening at once
_____ 15. to know (be aware of), past tense
_____ 16. that which grows on the top of one's head
_____ 17. a preposition describing a location
_____ 18. equitable, even-handed. also, pale or light colored
_____ 19. something recent; not old
_____ 20. a place that rents rooms to travelers
_____ 21. to take away
_____ 22. an attitude that is hardened against something

22   Made e with 1-2-3 Word Search Maker

HOMONYMS 21-30, PUZZLE 3

Use the clues to find the answers in the crossword puzzle.

ACROSS

2 equitable, even-handed. also, pale or light colored
4 24-hour periods
7 that which grows on the top of one's head
10 something recent; not old
12 to hold back something
13 to take away
14 another name for a wildebeest
17 something used to lure something else
18 the cost of transportation
19 to know (be aware of), past tense
20 a place that rents rooms to travelers

DOWN

1 a hardened, thickened area of skin
3 a festival, with many things happening at once
4 confuse
5 old term for "over there"
6 an attitude that is hardened against someone or something
8 allow or agree to
9 to walk in shallow water
11 to check on one's weight, past tense
15 a rabbit
16 a wide opening of the mouth that occurs when one is sleepy
20 a preposition describing a location

HOMONYMS 21-30, PUZZLE 4

Use the clues to find the answers in the word search puzzle. Words can be found horizontally, vertically, or diagonally.

```
Y  R  K  W  D  A  Y  S  V  F  R
F  O  T  E  G  S  T  I  A  B  D
A  D  N  N  U  N  E  I  T  E  I
I  E  A  L  J  X  R  K  H  N  R
R  D  L  Z  C  E  R  G  N  I  S
G  A  Q  E  E  U  I  X  A  N  U
C  W  P  J  H  E  N  H  C  K  O
E  T  R  G  W  A  G  G  C  N  L
V  T  Y  A  W  N  R  Y  E  E  L
I  N  A  E  R  A  F  E  P  W  A
R  Y  P  B  R  W  H  K  T  W  C
```

_____ 1. to walk in shallow water
_____ 2. another name for a wildebeest
_____ 3. a festival, with many things happening at once
_____ 4. confuse
_____ 5. a rabbit
_____ 6. 24-hour periods
_____ 7. something used to lure something else
_____ 8. the cost of transportation
_____ 9. to hold back something
_____ 10. a hardened, thickened area of skin
_____ 11. allow or agree to
_____ 12. old term for "over there"
_____ 13. to know (be aware of), past tense
_____ 14. that which grows on the top of one's head
_____ 15. an attitude that is hardened against something
_____ 16. a preposition describing a location
_____ 17. a wide opening of the mouth when one is sleepy
_____ 18. equitable, even-handed. also, pale or light colored
_____ 19 something recent; not old
_____ 20. a place that rents rooms to travelers
_____ 21. to take away
_____ 22. to check on one's weight, past tense

24   Made e with 1-2-3 Word Search Maker

LESSON 4: HOMONYMS 31 – 40

31.	Knight: Night:	A trusted warrior in medieval Europe. Evening, after sunset.
32.	Lair: Layer:	A home or den. A hideout/hangout. One thing placed directly on top of another.
33.	Mail: Male:	Letters, packages. To send or transmit. A man.
34.	None: Nun:	Not any; no one. A religious woman dedicated to her God through a restricted lifestyle.
35.	One: Won:	Single. To have a victory, past tense.
36.	Pail: Pale:	A bucket. Missing some color.
37.	Racket: Racquet:	Noise or clamor. Illegal enterprise. Tool used in tennis and badminton.
38.	Sawed: Sod:	To saw, past tense. Grass with matted roots.
39.	Tail: Tale:	The end of something. A story.
40.	Vary: Very:	Differ. An adverb showing emphasis.

Assignment Schedule for One-Year Course

Monday:	Give students the list above. Have them copy Groups 31-33 into their spelling notebook.
Tuesday:	Have students copy Groups 34-36 into their spelling notebook. Do Puzzle 1.
Wednesday:	Have students copy Groups 37-38 into their spelling notebook. Do Puzzle 2.
Thursday:	Have students copy Groups 39-40 into their spelling notebook. Do Puzzle 3.
Friday:	Do Puzzle 4 – without the lesson sheet or spelling notebook.
Friday fun:	Write a quatrain (a four-line poem) with some of these homonyms.

Assignment Schedule for Two-Year Course

Monday:	Give students the list above. Have them copy Groups 31-32 into their spelling notebook.
Tuesday:	Have students copy Groups 33-34 into their spelling notebook.
Wednesday:	Have students copy Groups 35-36 into their spelling notebook.
Thursday:	Have students copy Groups 37-38 into their spelling notebook.
Friday:	Have students copy Groups 39-40 into their spelling notebook.
Monday:	Do Puzzle 1.
Tuesday:	Do Puzzle 2.
Wednesday:	Do Puzzle 3.
Thursday:	Do Puzzle 4. – without the lesson sheet or spelling notebook.
Friday fun:	Write a quatrain (a four-line poem) with some of these homonyms.

HOMONYMS 31-40, PUZZLE 1

Use the clues to find the answers in the crossword puzzle.

ACROSS

1 grass with matted roots
2 one thing placed directly on top of another
6 to have a victory, past tense
8 noise or clamor; illegal enterprise
10 differ
11 not any; no one
12 evening, after sunset
13 a man
14 missing some color
15 a story

DOWN

1 to saw, past tense
2 a home or den. a hideout/hangout
3 tool used in tennis and badminton
4 single
5 a trusted warrior in medieval Europe
7 a religious woman who lives a restricted lifestyle
9 the end of something
10 an adverb showing emphasis
13 letters, packages. to send or transmit
14 a bucket

HOMONYMS 31-40, PUZZLE 2

Use the clues to find the answers in the word search puzzle. Words can be found horizontally, vertically, or diagonally.

```
T D N J Q R A C Q U E T
R O N S R Y M H P M T T
W Y O M Y A T Y P A I L
R D C R L T H D E W A S
A L A E H C G M Y L T M
C V W G R G I A R B M N
K C I M K C N I D V K F
E N O N L N K L L A I R
T L K W P A U V T R T E
E K I M W A Y N E L J L
N V H A K D L E Y R G A
O Z G R T P Y E R R Y T
```

_____ 1. missing some color
_____ 2. a story
_____ 3. a trusted warrior in medieval Europe
_____ 4. single
_____ 5. a man
_____ 6. the end of something
_____ 7. a bucket
_____ 8. to saw, past tense
_____ 9. an adverb showing emphasis
_____ 10. evening, after sunset
_____ 11. tool used in tennis and badminton
_____ 12. a home or den
_____ 13. to have a victory, past tense
_____ 14. letters, packages; to send or transmit
_____ 15. differ
_____ 16. noise or clamor
_____ 17. not any; no one
_____ 18. grass with matted roots
_____ 19. one thing placed directly on top of another
_____ 20. a religious woman who lives a restricted lifestyle

28   Made with 1-2-3 Word Search Maker

HOMONYMS 31-40, PUZZLE 3

Use the clues to find the answers in the crossword puzzle.

ACROSS

3 letters, packages. to send or transmit
7 missing some color
8 the end of something
9 tool used in tennis and badminton
11 an adverb showing emphasis
12 not any; no one
14 one thing placed directly on top of another
15 evening, after sunset
16 to have a victory, past tense
17 grass with matted roots

DOWN

1 a bucket
2 single
4 a home or den. a hideout/hangout
5 a man
6 noise or clamor; illegal enterprise
8 a story
10 a trusted warrior in medieval Europe
11 differ
13 to saw, past tense
15 a religious woman who lives a restricted lifestyle

HOMONYMS 31-40, PUZZLE 4

Use the clues to find the answers in the word search puzzle. Words can be found horizontally, vertically, or diagonally.

```
Q  B  S  C  T  N  T  M  S  M  M
M  O  W  H  O  A  H  T  A  E  A
D  L  G  W  L  P  N  H  W  N  I
R  I  T  E  N  O  N  G  E  O  L
N  A  H  E  L  M  V  I  D  C  F
M  T  X  M  U  A  N  N  N  Y  Y
F  P  A  H  M  Q  Y  K  R  U  D
K  L  A  I  R  Q  C  E  R  K  N
E  K  T  L  R  B  V  A  R  Y  F
J  Z  J  T  E  K  C  A  R  H  V
X  Y  R  A  V  L  P  A  I  L  H
```

_____ 1. a story
_____ 2. noise or clamor
_____ 3. a trusted warrior in medieval Europe
_____ 4. single
_____ 5. differ
_____ 6. a man
_____ 7. missing some color
_____ 8. the end of something
_____ 9. to saw, past tense
_____ 10. an adverb showing emphasis
_____ 11. evening, after sunset
_____ 12. tool used in tennis and badminton
_____ 13. one thing placed directly on top of another
_____ 14. a home or den
_____ 15. a bucket
_____ 16. to have a victory, past tense
_____ 17. letters, packages; to send or transmit
_____ 18. not any; no one
_____ 19. grass with matted roots
_____ 20. a religious woman who lives a restricted lifestyle

Made with 1-2-3 Word Search Maker

LESSON 5: HOMONYMS 41 – 50

41.	Wail: Wale: Whale:	To cry aloud. A ridge of fabric. A skin welt. A large, sea-dwelling mammal.
42.	Yoke: Yolk:	Wooden harness used to group animals to work together. The yellow part of an egg.
43.	Adds: Ads Adz:	To put in, insert. To tally or total up. Slang for advertisements A tool that is similar to an ax.
44.	Ball: Bawl:	A sphere, like a basketball or softball. The sound made by a calf.
45.	Can't Cant	Contraction for *can* and *not*. Lean to one side.
46.	Dear: Deer:	Something or someone important to a person. An antlered mammal. Venison.
47.	Fairy: Ferry:	A tiny being who flies and has magical powers. A commuter boat. To transport or carry.
48.	Gorilla: Guerilla:	Large ape-like mammal. A military-type fighter who is not in an official army.
49.	Half: Halve: Have:	One of two equal parts. To separate something into two equal parts. To possess something. *Half is a near homonym.*
50.	Instance: Instants:	An example. Plural form of instant, a moment.

Assignment Schedule for One-Year Course

Monday:	Give students the list above. Have them copy Groups 41-43 into their spelling notebook.
Tuesday:	Have students copy Groups 44-46 into their spelling notebook. Do Puzzle 1.
Wednesday:	Have students copy Groups 47-48 into their spelling notebook. Do Puzzle 2.
Thursday:	Have students copy Groups 49-50 into their spelling notebook. Do Puzzle 3.
Friday:	Do Puzzle 4 – without the lesson sheet or spelling notebook.
Friday fun:	Write a paragraph with as many of these homonyms as possible. This list includes fairy and several animals; you might want to write about one or more of them.

Assignment Schedule for Two-Year Course

Monday:	Give students the list above. Have them copy Groups 41-42 into their spelling notebook.
Tuesday:	Have students copy Groups 43-44 into their spelling notebook.
Wednesday:	Have students copy Groups 45-46 into their spelling notebook.
Thursday:	Have students copy Groups 47-48 into their spelling notebook.
Friday:	Have students copy Groups 49-50 into their spelling notebook.
Monday:	Do Puzzle 1.
Tuesday:	Do Puzzle 2.
Wednesday:	Do Puzzle 3.
Thursday:	Do Puzzle 4. – without the lesson sheet or spelling notebook.
Friday fun:	Write a paragraph with as many of these homonyms as possible. This list includes fairy and several animals; you might want to write about one or more of them.

HOMONYMS 41-50, PUZZLE 1

Use the clues to find the answers in the crossword puzzle.

ACROSS

4 an antlered mammal; venison
5 the yellow part of an egg
7 a ridge of fabric; a skin welt
9 the sound made by a calf
13 something or someone important to a person
15 plural form of instant; moments
17 a large, sea-dwelling mammal
18 a sphere, like a basketball or softball
19 to possess something
21 an example
22 a tiny being who flies and has magical powers

DOWN

1 large ape-like mammal
2 one of two equal parts
3 a commuter boat. to transport or carry
5 wooden harness used to group animals to work together
6 contraction for can and not
8 to put in, insert. to tally or total up
10 to cry aloud
11 to separate something into two equal parts
12 a military-type fighter who is not in an official army
14 lean to one side
16 slang for advertisements
20 a tool that is similar to an ax

HOMONYMS 41-50, PUZZLE 2

Use the clues to find the answers in the word search puzzle. Words can be found horizontally, vertically, or diagonally.

```
H  A  L  V  E  M  H  L  C  A  N  '  T  L
N  I  W  J  L  Q  X  A  J  J  K  A  C  X
Q  N  Z  F  C  A  G  E  V  Z  T  L  V  N
M  S  M  T  D  A  L  M  L  E  Y  L  Y  I
K  T  M  D  H  A  N  W  T  M  Y  I  O  N
D  A  S  R  W  T  A  T  G  T  K  R  L  S
E  N  N  K  B  B  Y  C  Y  G  R  O  K  T
A  T  W  H  A  L  E  O  U  R  R  G  C  A
R  S  R  L  N  Y  H  E  K  L  R  F  D  N
T  L  L  S  D  A  R  L  F  E  D  E  C  C
M  I  N  R  P  I  G  L  C  X  E  M  F  E
Y  A  W  M  L  F  A  A  Z  R  W  W  T  R
D  W  X  L  Z  H  Y  B  M  D  Z  H  B  N
L  T  A  Y  R  I  A  F  L  R  A  M  R  J
```

_____ 1. to cry aloud
_____ 2. slang for advertisements
_____ 3. the yellow part of an egg
_____ 4. to put in, insert. to tally or total up
_____ 5. an antlered mammal; venison
_____ 6. a sphere, like a basketball or softball
_____ 7. large ape-like mammal
_____ 8. the sound made by a calf
_____ 9. a ridge of fabric; a skin welt
_____ 10. contraction for _can_ and _not_
_____ 11. something or someone important to a person
_____ 12. a tiny being who flies and has magical powers
_____ 13. a large, sea-dwelling mammal
_____ 14. one of two equal parts
_____ 15. a commuter boat. to transport or carry
_____ 16. lean to one side
_____ 17. a military-type fighter who is not in an official army
_____ 18. to separate something into two equal parts
_____ 19. a tool that is similar to an ax
_____ 20. to possess something
_____ 21. an example
_____ 22. wooden harness used to group animals to work together
_____ 23. plural form of instant; moments

HOMONYMS 41-50, PUZZLE 3

Use the clues to find the answers in the crossword puzzle.

ACROSS

3 one of two equal parts
5 contraction for can and not
6 to possess something
8 plural form of instant; moments
10 wooden harness used to group animals to work together
12 an antlered mammal; venison
14 to put in, insert. to tally or total up
16 a commuter boat. to transport or carry
17 a tool that is similar to an ax
18 a ridge of fabric; a skin welt
19 the sound made by a calf
20 a sphere, like a basketball or softball

DOWN

1 the yellow part of an egg
2 a large, sea-dwelling mammal
4 a tiny being who flies and has magical powers
5 lean to one side
7 a military-type fighter who is not in an official army
8 an example
9 to separate something into two equal parts
11 slang for advertisements
13 large ape-like mammal
15 something or someone important to a person
18 to cry aloud

Made with Crossword Weaver

HOMONYMS 41-50, PUZZLE 4

Use the clues to find the answers in the word search puzzle. Words can be found horizontally, vertically, or diagonally.

```
X  B  L  M  G  Q  Z  D  Y  H  A  L  V  E
X  G  W  J  F  U  E  C  O  Y  N  T  N  F
Q  D  C  E  L  E  E  V  L  T  O  N  T  L
C  E  L  A  R  R  N  R  K  Z  D  K  W  R
B  A  K  L  N  R  P  W  I  Z  V  A  E  H
W  R  K  L  R  T  S  D  A  L  B  Y  T  A
Y  R  I  A  F  T  T  W  H  A  L  E  K  V
M  N  P  B  M  N  V  L  X  K  G  A  N  E
X  Y  R  I  N  S  T  A  N  T  S  L  F  Z
B  B  R  N  A  L  L  K  X  D  L  M  L
Y  G  D  R  D  C  A  N  '  T  A  I  F  I
Y  R  D  D  E  X  D  K  Z  H  W  R  M  A
V  T  S  B  P  F  Q  B  V  D  L  O  C  W
K  R  E  C  N  A  T  S  N  I  A  G  B  D
```

_____ 1. to cry aloud
_____ 2. an example
_____ 3. slang for advertisements
_____ 4. to put in, insert. to tally or total up
_____ 5. an antlered mammal; venison
_____ 6. a sphere, like a basketball or softball
_____ 7. something or someone important to a person
_____ 8. large ape-like mammal
_____ 9. the sound made by a calf
_____ 10. a ridge of fabric; a skin welt
_____ 11. a commuter boat. to transport or carry
_____ 12. contraction for *can* and *not*
_____ 13. a tiny being who flies and has magical powers
_____ 14. a large, sea-dwelling mammal
_____ 15. to possess something
_____ 16. one of two equal parts
_____ 17. a military-type fighter who is not in an official army
_____ 18. the yellow part of an egg
_____ 19. to separate something into two equal parts
_____ 20. lean to one side
_____ 21. a tool that is similar to an ax
_____ 22. wooden harness used to group animals to work together
_____ 23. plural form of instant; moments

LESSON 6: HOMONYMS 51 – 60

51.	Knot: Not: Naught:	To tie or loop. To tether or secure. An adverb that negates something. Nothing, zip, zero, nil.
52.	Lay: Lei:	To place something on a surface. A garland of flowers, typically associated with Hawaii.
53.	Main: Maine: Mane:	Major, most important. Northernmost state on the East Coast. Curls; extra hair found on the head and shoulders of a horse or a male lion.
54.	Ordinance: Ordnance:	Rule or law. Weapons.
55.	Pain: Pane:	Discomfort. A sheet of glass.
56	Rain: Reign: Rein:	Water that falls from the sky. To pour or shower. To rule. Time in office/power. (Match the "g" with "regal" or "government.") Bridle, harness, or strap. (Match the "in" with a strap that can be measured in *in*ches.)
57.	Scene: Seen:	Setting, location. To see, participle.
58.	Tare: Tear:	An old word for a weed. To rip or slash. A slit or split.
59.	Verses: Versus:	Groups of lines in a song or poem. Against.
60.	Waist: Waste:	The place about the middle of an object; it can be measured in inches (match it up with the "i" for inches). Trash (match it up with the "e" for environment).

Assignment Schedule for One-Year Course

Monday:	Give students the list above. Have them copy Groups 51-53 into their spelling notebook.
Tuesday:	Have students copy Groups 54-56 into their spelling notebook. Do Puzzle 1.
Wednesday:	Have students copy Groups 57-58 into their spelling notebook. Do Puzzle 2.
Thursday:	Have students copy Groups 59-60 into their spelling notebook. Do Puzzle 3.
Friday:	Do Puzzle 4 – without the lesson sheet or spelling notebook.
Friday fun:	Write a newspaper article with as many of these homonyms as possible.

Assignment Schedule for Two-Year Course

Monday:	Give students the list above. Have them copy Groups 51-52 into their spelling notebook.
Tuesday:	Have students copy Groups 53-54 into their spelling notebook.
Wednesday:	Have students copy Groups 55-56 into their spelling notebook.
Thursday:	Have students copy Groups 57-58 into their spelling notebook.
Friday:	Have students copy Groups 59-60 into their spelling notebook.
Monday:	Do Puzzle 1.
Tuesday:	Do Puzzle 2.
Wednesday:	Do Puzzle 3.
Thursday:	Do Puzzle 4. – without the lesson sheet or spelling notebook.
Friday fun:	Write a newspaper article with as many of these homonyms as possible.

Made with Crossword Weaver

HOMONYMS 51-60, PUZZLE 1

Use the clues to find the answers in the crossword puzzle.

ACROSS

3 to see, participle
4 an adverb that negates something
6 to tie or loop. to tether or secure
10 an old word for a weed
12 the place about the middle of an object
14 to place something on a surface
15 northernmost state on the east coast
16 groups of lines in a song or poem
20 a garland of flowers, typically associated with Hawaii
21 setting, location
22 nothing, zip, zero, nil

DOWN

1 major, most important
2 bridle, harness, or strap
5 rule or law
7 weapons
8 against
9 to rule; time in office/power
11 a sheet of glass
13 discomfort
15 extra hair found on the head & shoulders of a horse or a male lion
17 water that falls from the sky; to pour or shower
18 trash
19 to rip or slash. a slit or split

HOMONYMS 51-60, PUZZLE 2

Use the clues to find the answers in the word search puzzle. Words can be found horizontally, vertically, or diagonally.

```
Y  Y  P  A  I  N  V  E  R  S  U  S  Z
J  X  C  N  W  K  E  N  I  A  M  T  L
E  T  E  A  R  R  R  P  J  V  R  Z  T
D  N  S  P  E  N  A  U  G  H  T  E  N
L  T  E  I  A  M  D  Z  B  B  C  E  E
E  A  G  C  E  N  G  D  K  N  K  C  E
N  N  Y  V  S  N  E  W  A  N  M  N  S
D  X  Z  M  E  E  A  N  F  W  R  A  H
G  H  A  M  R  R  D  M  X  A  A  N  L
W  I  B  A  T  R  S  C  K  I  I  I  T
N  V  T  O  O  L  D  E  M  S  N  D  O
N  M  N  G  J  E  Q  K  S  T  M  R  N
D  D  G  Y  N  I  E  R  H  Y  Y  O  K
```

_____ 1. trash
_____ 2. to tie or loop. to tether or secure
_____ 3. discomfort
_____ 4. an adverb that negates something
_____ 5. to place something on a surface
_____ 6. against
_____ 7. an old word for a weed
_____ 8. major, most important
_____ 9. northernmost state on the east coast
_____ 10. rule or law
_____ 11. weapons
_____ 12. a sheet of glass
_____ 13. water that falls from the sky; to pour or shower
_____ 14. nothing, zip, zero, nil
_____ 15. bridle, harness, or strap
_____ 16. setting, location
_____ 17. to see, participle
_____ 18. to rip or slash. a slit or split
_____ 19. groups of lines in a song or poem
_____ 20. to rule; time in office/power
_____ 21. the place about the middle of an object
_____ 22. extra hair found on the head & shoulders of a horse
_____ 23. a garland of flowers, typically associated with Hawaii

HOMONYMS 51-60, PUZZLE 3

Use the clues to find the answers in the crossword puzzle.

ACROSS

4 discomfort
8 weapons
9 to rule; time in office/power
10 a garland of flowers, typically associated with Hawaii
11 a sheet of glass
12 against
19 an old word for a weed
20 rule or law
21 setting, location
22 nothing, zip, zero, nil

DOWN

1 trash
2 to tie or loop. to tether or secure
3 bridle, harness, or strap
5 extra hair found on the head & shoulders of a horse or a male lion
6 groups of lines in a song or poem
7 major, most important
10 to place something on a surface
13 water that falls from the sky; to pour or shower
14 northernmost state on the east coast
15 the place about the middle of an object
16 to rip or slash. a slit or split
17 an adverb that negates something
18 to see, participle

41

HOMONYMS 51-60, PUZZLE 4

Use the clues to find the answers in the word search puzzle. Words can be found horizontally, vertically, or diagonally.

```
K  Q  E  Q  W  R  P  A  I  N  N  F  E
N  Z  V  N  K  G  L  M  M  M  B  E  C
D  E  J  E  E  W  N  I  E  R  C  E  N
T  J  N  M  R  C  Z  Z  M  N  R  T  A
O  M  R  A  C  S  S  X  A  C  D  S  N
N  L  Y  D  M  M  E  N  I  A  M  A  I
K  E  M  K  A  W  D  S  R  L  T  W  D
Y  I  B  I  E  R  A  E  M  O  V  V  R
L  L  N  R  O  K  I  I  N  X  E  N  O
N  A  A  P  Y  G  P  K  S  G  R  R  N
E  T  Y  R  N  F  Z  A  N  T  S  A  L
E  N  A  U  G  H  T  P  N  H  U  I  G
S  W  L  T  E  A  R  C  Z  E  S  N  K
```

_____ 1. trash
_____ 2. weapons
_____ 3. to tie or loop. to tether or secure
_____ 4. discomfort
_____ 5. against
_____ 6. an old word for a weed
_____ 7. major, most important
_____ 8. northernmost state on the east coast
_____ 9. rule or law
_____ 10. the place about the middle of an object
_____ 11. a sheet of glass
_____ 12. nothing, zip, zero, nil
_____ 13. bridle, harness, or strap
_____ 14. an adverb that negates something
_____ 15. to rule; time in office/power
_____ 16. setting, location
_____ 17. to see, participle
_____ 18. to rip or slash. a slit or split
_____ 19. to place something on a surface
_____ 20. groups of lines in a song or poem
_____ 21. extra hair found on the head of a horse
_____ 22. water that falls from the sky; to pour or shower
_____ 23. a garland of flowers, typically associated with Hawaii

42   Made with 1-2-3 Word Search Maker

LESSON 7: HOMONYMS 61 – 70

61.	Yore: You're: Your:	The old days. Contraction of the words *you* and *are*. Possessive pronoun meaning that you own something.
62.	-Ade: Aid: Aide:	Suffix meaning a sweet, fruity drink. To help. A person who helps.
63.	Band: Banned:	Group, crowd. Music group. A strip or belt. Barred, excluded, expelled. Forbidden, illegal.
64.	Canvas: Canvass:	A heavy fabric. To travel around an area asking people for something, usually information.
65.	Den: Din:	A small communal living area. A great deal of noise.
66.	Faun: Fawn:	A mythological creature similar to a satyr. A young deer; to kiss up to someone.
67.	Grate: Great:	To cut into small, thin strips. The covering over a hole. Excellent or large.
68.	Hardy: Hearty:	Resilient; tough; strong. Vigorous/energetic. Warm/cheerful. Filling/nourishing.
69.	It's: Its:	Contraction for *it* and *is*. Possessive pronoun showing ownership by something not human.
70.	Know: No:	To have information. Opposite of yes.

Assignment Schedule for One-Year Course

Monday:	Give students the list above. Have them copy Groups 61-63 into their spelling notebook.
Tuesday:	Have students copy Groups 64-66 into their spelling notebook. Do Puzzle 1.
Wednesday:	Have students copy Groups 67-68 into their spelling notebook. Do Puzzle 2.
Thursday:	Have students copy Groups 69-70 into their spelling notebook. Do Puzzle 3.
Friday:	Do Puzzle 4 – without the lesson sheet or spelling notebook.
Friday fun:	Use as many of these homonyms as possible to tell about a painting or a picture.

Assignment Schedule for Two-Year Course

Monday:	Give students the list above. Have them copy Groups 61-62 into their spelling notebook.
Tuesday:	Have students copy Groups 63-64 into their spelling notebook.
Wednesday:	Have students copy Groups 65-66 into their spelling notebook.
Thursday:	Have students copy Groups 67-68 into their spelling notebook.
Friday:	Have students copy Groups 69-70 into their spelling notebook.
Monday:	Do Puzzle 1.
Tuesday:	Do Puzzle 2.
Wednesday:	Do Puzzle 3.
Thursday:	Do Puzzle 4. – without the lesson sheet or spelling notebook.
Friday fun:	Use as many of these homonyms as possible to tell about a painting or a picture.

HOMONYMS 61-70, PUZZLE 1

Use the clues to find the answers in the crossword puzzle.

ACROSS

1 vigorous/energetic; warm/cheerful; filling/nourishing
3 excellent or large
4 the old days
7 to cut into small, thin strips; the covering over a hole
10 to help
11 possessive pronoun showing ownership by something not human
12 barred, excluded, expelled. forbidden, illegal
15 a mythological creature similar to a satyr
16 to have information
17 a heavy fabric
18 opposite of yes

DOWN

1 resilient; tough; strong
2 contraction of the words you and are
4 possessive pronoun meaning that you own something
5 a small communal living area
6 group, crowd; music group; a strip or belt
8 a person who helps
9 to travel around an area asking people for information
11 contraction for it and is
13 suffix meaning a sweet, fruity drink
14 a great deal of noise
15 a young deer; to kiss up to someone

45

HOMONYMS 61-70, PUZZLE 2

Use the clues to find the answers in the word search puzzle. Words can be found horizontally, vertically, or diagonally.

```
Q  S  S  A  V  N  A  C  L  T  Q
Y  V  K  T  A  E  R  G  D  I  N
M  F  T  A  R  E  F  C  M  S  Y
L  T  I  '  T  R  Y  A  G  A  T
M  D  U  K  G  O  A  D  U  V  R
E  O  D  R  N  Y  C  D  R  N  A
Y  T  A  E  T  O  R  A  E  A  E
I  T  S  S  N  N  W  I  F  C  H
E  J  '  Z  E  N  H  D  A  M  N
Z  T  N  D  D  N  A  B  W  Q  O
I  K  Y  O  U  R  P  B  N  V  F
```

_____ 1. the old days

_____ 2. a heavy fabric

_____ 3. to help

_____ 4. contraction of the words *you* and *are*

_____ 5. excellent or large

_____ 6. possessive pronoun meaning that you own something

_____ 7. suffix meaning a sweet, fruity drink

_____ 8. opposite of yes

_____ 9. barred, excluded, expelled. forbidden, illegal

_____ 10. contraction for *it* and *is*

_____ 11. a person who helps

_____ 12. to travel around an area asking people for information

_____ 13. a small communal living area

_____ 14. resilient; tough; strong

_____ 15. a great deal of noise

_____ 16. a mythological creature similar to a satyr

_____ 17. to have information

_____ 18. to cut into small, thin strips; the covering over a hole

_____ 19. group, crowd; music group; a strip or belt

_____ 20. vigorous/energetic; warm/cheerful; filling/nourishing

_____ 21. possessive pronoun showing ownership by something not human

_____ 22. a young deer; to kiss up to someone

HOMONYMS 61-70, PUZZLE 3

Use the clues to find the answers in the crossword puzzle.

ACROSS

1 a mythological creature similar to a satyr
3 suffix meaning a sweet, fruity drink
8 to cut into small, thin strips; the covering over a hole
9 possessive pronoun meaning that you own something
10 a heavy fabric
11 opposite of yes
12 group, crowd; music group; a strip or belt
13 a young deer; to kiss up to someone
14 contraction of the words you and are
16 possessive pronoun showing ownership by something not human
17 a small communal living area

DOWN

2 to help
3 a person who helps
4 contraction for it and is
5 resilient; tough; strong
6 excellent or large
7 to have information
9 the old days
10 to travel around an area asking people for information
12 barred, excluded, expelled, forbidden, illegal
15 a great deal of noise

47 Made with Crossword Weaver

HOMONYMS 61-70, PUZZLE 4

Use the clues to find the answers in the word search puzzle. Words can be found horizontally, vertically, or diagonally.

```
J  D  N  A  B  N  T  D  I  N  H
P  T  E  T  A  R  G  A  E  T  O
N  P  A  M  P  F  M  R  D  L  F
J  D  Y  E  A  N  '  Y  A  E  A
C  S  E  W  R  U  E  D  I  W  U
H  A  N  N  O  G  R  R  D  F  N
E  V  N  Y  N  N  O  A  H  J  S
A  N  G  V  E  A  Y  H  A  T  X
R  A  R  D  A  D  B  I  I  Q  C
T  C  T  R  B  S  D  Y  O  U  R
Y  K  N  O  W  E  S  S  '  T  I
```

_____ 1. to help
_____ 2. the old days
_____ 3. a heavy fabric
_____ 4. excellent or large
_____ 5. possessive pronoun meaning that you own something
_____ 6. suffix meaning a sweet, fruity drink
_____ 7. a mythological creature similar to a satyr
_____ 8. opposite of yes
_____ 9. contraction for *it* and *is*
_____ 10. a person who helps
_____ 11. to travel around an area asking people for information
_____ 12. a small communal living area
_____ 13. contraction of the words *you* and *are*
_____ 14. resilient; tough; strong
_____ 15. a young deer; to kiss up to someone
_____ 16. a great deal of noise
_____ 17. to have information
_____ 18. to cut into small, thin strips; the covering over a hole
_____ 19. barred, excluded, expelled. forbidden, illegal
_____ 20. group, crowd; music group; a strip or belt
_____ 21. vigorous/energetic; warm/cheerful; filling/nourishing
_____ 22. possessive pronoun showing ownership by something not human

LESSON 8: HOMONYMS 71 – 80

71.	Lays: Laze:	To place something in a resting position. To take it easy, relax, and do no work.
72.	Maize: Maze:	Corn. A puzzle that an individual walks through. Confusion/muddle.
73.	Pair: Pare: Pear:	Two things grouped together. To peel down in thin strips. A bell-shaped fruit.
74.	Raise: Rays: Raze:	To lift up, increase, or improve. Geometry: straight lines that emanate from a point. Beams of light from the sun. To cut down to ground level, demolish, annihilate.
75.	Sea: See:	A good-sized body of water that is smaller than an ocean. To use the eyes to observe things.
76.	Tea: Tee:	A hot drink brewed from tasty leaves. The small wooden peg that holds a golf ball for a player.
77.	Wait: Weight:	To pause. Heaviness, mass, burden. Can also mean influence or emphasis.
78.	You'll: Yule:	Contraction for *you* and *will*. Related to Christmas.
79.	Affect: Effect:	To influence, shape, or change. Result or outcome. To achieve or cause.
80.	Bare: Bear:	Without appropriate covering. A large, furry mammal with fearsome claws & teeth.

Assignment Schedule for One-Year Course

Monday:	Give students the list above. Have them copy Groups 71-73 into their spelling notebook.
Tuesday:	Have students copy Groups 74-76 into their spelling notebook. Do Puzzle 1.
Wednesday:	Have students copy Groups 77-78 into their spelling notebook. Do Puzzle 2.
Thursday:	Have students copy Groups 79-80 into their spelling notebook. Do Puzzle 3.
Friday:	Do Puzzle 4 – without the lesson sheet or spelling notebook.
Friday fun:	Using some of these homonyms, write a limerick.

Assignment Schedule for Two-Year Course

Monday:	Give students the list above. Have them copy Groups 71-72 into their spelling notebook.
Tuesday:	Have students copy Groups 73-74 into their spelling notebook.
Wednesday:	Have students copy Groups 75-76 into their spelling notebook.
Thursday:	Have students copy Groups 77-78 into their spelling notebook.
Friday:	Have students copy Groups 79-80 into their spelling notebook.
Monday:	Do Puzzle 1.
Tuesday:	Do Puzzle 2.
Wednesday:	Do Puzzle 3.
Thursday:	Do Puzzle 4. – without the lesson sheet or spelling notebook.
Friday fun:	Using some of these homonyms, write a limerick.

HOMONYMS 71-80, PUZZLE 1

Use the clues to find the answers in the crossword puzzle.

ACROSS

1 to pause
4 to place something in a resting position
5 beams of light from the sun
7 to use the eyes to observe things
9 corn
10 without appropriate covering
11 a bell-shaped fruit
13 contraction for you and will
15 to take it easy, relax, and do no work
16 result or outcome; to achieve or cause
18 heaviness; can also mean influence or emphasis
19 a large, furry mammal with fearsome claws & teeth

DOWN

2 a hot drink brewed from tasty leaves
3 to lift up, increase, or improve
5 to cut down to ground level, demolish, annihilate
6 a good-sized body of water that is smaller than an ocean
8 two things grouped together
11 to peel down in thin strips
12 to influence, shape, or change
13 related to Christmas
14 a puzzle that an individual walks through
17 the small wooden peg that holds a golf ball for a player

HOMONYMS 71-80, PUZZLE 2

Use the clues to find the answers in the word search puzzle. Words can be found horizontally, vertically, or diagonally.

```
R  T  I  A  W  X  B  L  N  M  R  L
R  E  R  S  M  D  T  E  E  X  S  L
M  R  F  Y  B  J  E  L  A  E  Y  '
C  A  T  A  J  Y  U  S  Z  R  A  U
P  B  Y  L  T  Y  C  A  I  X  R  O
T  M  A  I  Z  E  R  P  X  A  W  Y
R  H  L  P  Z  W  A  D  T  Y  R  L
M  R  G  A  N  R  T  C  R  A  E  P
S  A  L  I  E  E  E  S  E  A  N  T
R  E  Z  R  E  F  Y  Q  K  K  F  E
R  N  E  E  F  W  Q  L  W  R  H  A
G  B  G  E  T  A  F  F  E  C  T  T
```

_____ 1. to pause
_____ 2. to place something in a resting position
_____ 3. corn
_____ 4. to peel down in thin strips
_____ 5. without appropriate covering
_____ 6. a hot drink brewed from tasty leaves
_____ 7. a bell-shaped fruit
_____ 8. to lift up, increase, or improve
_____ 9. beams of light from the sun
_____ 10. to cut down to ground level, demolish, annihilate
_____ 11. a good-sized body of water that is smaller than an ocean
_____ 12. result or outcome; to achieve or cause
_____ 13. a puzzle that an individual walks through
_____ 14. to use the eyes to observe things
_____ 15. to take it easy, relax, and do no work
_____ 16. the small wooden peg that holds a golf ball for a player
_____ 17. heaviness; can also mean influence or emphasis
_____ 18. contraction for _you_ and _will_
_____ 19. two things grouped together
_____ 20. related to Christmas
_____ 21. to influence, shape, or change
_____ 22. a large, furry mammal with fearsome claws & teeth

HOMONYMS 71-80, PUZZLE 3

Use the clues to find the answers in the crossword puzzle.

ACROSS

2 heaviness; can also mean influence or emphasis
4 to peel down in thin strips
5 a good-sized body of water that is smaller than an ocean
8 a bell-shaped fruit
9 without appropriate covering
10 beams of light from the sun
13 a puzzle that an individual walks through
15 to pause
16 a large, furry mammal with fearsome claws & teeth
18 to place something in a resting position
19 result or outcome; to achieve or cause
20 the small wooden peg that holds a golf ball for a player

DOWN

1 related to Christmas
3 a hot drink brewed from tasty leaves
4 two things grouped together
5 to use the eyes to observe things
6 to take it easy, relax, and do no work
7 corn
11 contraction for you and will
12 to lift up, increase, or improve
14 to influence, shape, or change
17 to cut down to ground level, demolish, annihilate

HOMONYMS 71-80, PUZZLE 4

Use the clues to find the answers in the word search puzzle. Words can be found horizontally, vertically, or diagonally.

```
E  B  V  E  R  S  E  A  K  G  P  Y
K  L  C  J  S  Y  T  T  I  A  W  S
V  M  U  S  B  I  T  F  L  K  G  Y
L  T  A  Y  E  E  A  B  Q  P  Y  A
T  E  Z  Z  E  E  N  R  A  E  E  L
C  A  Z  N  E  T  W  R  Z  F  Q  L
E  W  M  A  I  Z  E  A  F  T  L  B
F  S  R  P  D  F  L  E  H  '  K  R
F  Y  D  A  H  K  C  G  U  E  L  A
A  A  N  I  W  T  I  O  Z  G  D  E
W  R  L  R  B  E  Y  A  H  W  K  B
R  A  E  P  W  M  R  R  B  A  R  E
```

_____ 1. to place something in a resting position
_____ 2. corn
_____ 3. to peel down in thin strips
_____ 4. without appropriate covering
_____ 5. to pause
_____ 6. related to Christmas
_____ 7. to cut down to ground level, demolish, annihilate
_____ 8. a bell-shaped fruit
_____ 9. to lift up, increase, or improve
_____ 10. beams of light from the sun
_____ 11. a good-sized body of water that is smaller than an ocean
_____ 12. to take it easy, relax, and do no work
_____ 13. result or outcome; to achieve or cause
_____ 14. a puzzle that an individual walks through
_____ 15. a hot drink brewed from tasty leaves
_____ 16. to use the eyes to observe things
_____ 17. to influence, shape, or change
_____ 18. the small wooden peg that holds a golf ball for a player
_____ 19. heaviness; can also mean influence or emphasis
_____ 20. contraction for _you_ and _will_
_____ 21. two things grouped together
_____ 22. a large, furry mammal with fearsome claws & teeth

LESSON 9: HOMONYMS 81 – 90

81.	Capital: Capitol:	A seat of government. A building where the legislature meets.
82.	Desert: Dessert:	To abandon. A dry place with limited vegetation. A sweet food served after the main part of a meal. (Match up the "ss" with "super sweet.")
83.	Fawned: Fond:	To show affection in an insincere manner, past tense. To care for something.
84.	Groan: Grown:	A moan. An adult. To mature toward adulthood.
85.	Hart: Heart:	Old term for a deer. The organ that pumps blood. Feelings or emotions.
86.	Knows: Nose:	To have information. The feature in the center of one's face.
87.	Leach: Leech:	To remove from soil by percolation. A bloodsucking worm.
88.	Mall: Maul:	A large open area or a large place to shop. To mangle something.
89.	Passed: Past:	To go by, past tense. Preposition meaning to go by. Something that happened before the present.
90.	Rap: Wrap:	A sharp knock. A form of music. To cover with something.

Assignment Schedule for One-Year Course

Monday:	Give students the list above. Have them copy Groups 81-83 into their spelling notebook.
Tuesday:	Have students copy Groups 84-86 into their spelling notebook. Do Puzzle 1.
Wednesday:	Have students copy Groups 87-88 into their spelling notebook. Do Puzzle 2.
Thursday:	Have students copy Groups 89-90 into their spelling notebook. Do Puzzle 3.
Friday:	Do Puzzle 4 – without the lesson sheet or spelling notebook.
Friday fun:	This list has some great homonyms for a short story about a lion and/or a deer. Write an adventure story with some of these homonyms.

Assignment Schedule for Two-Year Course

Monday:	Give students the list above. Have them copy Groups 81-82 into their spelling notebook.
Tuesday:	Have students copy Groups 83-84 into their spelling notebook.
Wednesday:	Have students copy Groups 85-86 into their spelling notebook.
Thursday:	Have students copy Groups 87-88 into their spelling notebook.
Friday:	Have students copy Groups 89-90 into their spelling notebook.
Monday:	Do Puzzle 1.
Tuesday:	Do Puzzle 2.
Wednesday:	Do Puzzle 3.
Thursday:	Do Puzzle 4. – without the lesson sheet or spelling notebook.
Friday fun:	This list has some great homonyms for a short story about a lion and/or a deer. Write an adventure story with some of these homonyms.

HOMONYMS 81-90, PUZZLE 1

Use the clues to find the answers in the crossword puzzle.

ACROSS

3 a large open area or a large place to shop

6 to care for something

8 the organ that pumps blood; feelings or emotions

10 to abandon. a dry place with limited vegetation

11 a bloodsucking worm

13 preposition meaning to go by

14 to cover with something

16 an adult; to mature toward adulthood

17 a moan

18 to go by, past tense

DOWN

1 to mangle something

2 a seat of government

4 to have information

5 to remove from soil by percolation

7 the feature in the center of one's face

8 old term for a deer

9 a sharp knock. a form of music

10 a sweet food served after the main part of a meal

12 a building where the legislature meets

15 to show affection in an insincere manner, past tense

HOMONYMS 81-90, PUZZLE 2

Use the clues to find the answers in the word search puzzle. Words can be found horizontally, vertically, or diagonally.

```
F  L  D  N  N  A  O  R  G  W  P
A  P  U  E  O  W  R  A  P  A  D
W  A  L  A  S  S  O  L  R  L  E
N  S  A  T  M  S  E  R  O  R  S
E  T  T  D  J  E  E  T  G  D  S
D  H  I  Z  C  P  I  R  F  N  A
T  L  P  H  L  P  T  O  T  L  P
R  E  A  J  A  R  N  L  P  T  L
A  A  C  C  A  D  E  S  E  R  T
H  C  X  E  P  D  L  L  A  M  F
T  H  H  K  K  N  O  W  S  D  K
```

_____ 1. a seat of government
_____ 2. a moan
_____ 3. a bloodsucking worm
_____ 4. a building where the legislature meets
_____ 5. old term for a deer
_____ 6. to abandon. a dry place with limited vegetation
_____ 7. to mangle something
_____ 8. a sweet food served after the main part of a meal
_____ 9. to care for something
_____ 10. to cover with something
_____ 11. an adult; to mature toward adulthood
_____ 12. the organ that pumps blood; feelings or emotions
_____ 13. to have information
_____ 14. to remove from soil by percolation
_____ 15. a large open area or a large place to shop
_____ 16. to go by, past tense
_____ 17. to show affection in an insincere manner, past tense
_____ 18. preposition meaning to go by
_____ 19. the feature in the center of one's face
_____ 20. a sharp knock. a form of music

HOMONYMS 81-90, PUZZLE 3

Use the clues to find the answers in the crossword puzzle.

ACROSS

4 to show affection in an insincere manner, past tense

8 to cover with something

9 to go by, past tense

10 a sharp knock. a form of music

11 to remove from soil by percolation

13 preposition meaning to go by

14 a seat of government

17 old term for a deer

18 the feature in the center of one's face

19 a building where the legislature meets

DOWN

1 to have information

2 an adult; to mature toward adulthood

3 a moan

4 to care for something

5 to abandon. a dry place with limited vegetation

6 a sweet food served after the main part of a meal

7 to mangle something

12 the organ that pumps blood; feelings or emotions

15 a bloodsucking worm

16 a large open area or a large place to shop

HOMONYMS 81-90, PUZZLE 4

Use the clues to find the answers in the word search puzzle. Words can be found horizontally, vertically, or diagonally.

```
R  N  J  W  D  E  S  E  R  T  R  W
N  N  A  O  R  G  R  L  E  E  C  H
T  W  N  L  U  A  M  W  F  N  L  K
N  N  O  T  F  M  P  K  A  X  A  R
D  O  Z  R  N  F  L  L  W  L  T  P
T  E  S  P  G  D  O  T  N  E  I  A
R  S  S  E  E  T  R  F  E  A  P  R
A  W  A  S  I  A  O  C  D  C  A  K
H  F  S  P  E  N  K  M  Y  H  C  T
R  A  A  H  D  R  A  R  J  V  T  W
P  C  Z  R  M  L  T  M  M  L  H  D
L  K  G  R  L  G  N  K  N  O  W  S
```

_____ 1. a moan
_____ 2. a bloodsucking worm
_____ 3. to cover with something
_____ 4. a building where the legislature meets
_____ 5. to mangle something
_____ 6. to go by, past tense
_____ 7. old term for a deer
_____ 8. a seat of government
_____ 9. to care for something
_____ 10. an adult; to mature toward adulthood
_____ 11. the organ that pumps blood; feelings or emotions
_____ 12. to have information
_____ 13. to remove from soil by percolation
_____ 14. a large open area or a large place to shop
_____ 15. a sweet food served after the main part of a meal
_____ 16. to show affection in an insincere manner, past tense
_____ 17. to abandon. a dry place with limited vegetation
_____ 18. preposition meaning to go by
_____ 19. the feature in the center of one's face
_____ 20. a sharp knock. a form of music

Made with 1-2-3 Word Search Maker

LESSON 10: HOMONYMS 91 – 100

91.	Sear:	To quickly burn the exterior.
	Seer:	A prophet; one who sees. (Match the two "Es" with "eyes.")
92.	Team:	A group or band. A side or players.
	Teem:	To swarm or abound.
93.	Waive:	To give up something voluntarily.
	Wave:	Move the hand repeatedly as a signal. Moving ripple on the ocean.
94.	Ail:	To be ill or sick. To have trouble or pain.
	Ale:	An alcoholic beverage made from grain.
95.	Bar:	To prevent someone or something from passing.
	Barre:	A long horizontal pole that dancers use for stretching.
96.	Carat:	A unit of weight for precious stones.
	Carrot:	A long, orange vegetable.
	Karat:	A unit of weight for gold.
97.	Dew:	Moisture that accumulates on the ground over night.
	Do:	Verb meaning to accomplish something.
	Due:	Something owed at a particular time.
98.	Feat:	An accomplishment.
	Feet:	The body part we walk on.
99.	Guessed:	To form an opinion without knowing for certain, past tense.
	Guest:	One who visits another.
100.	Hay:	Cut grass that is used as food for cows and horses.
	Hey:	An interjection to call for a person's attention; a greeting.

Assignment Schedule for One-Year Course

Monday:	Give students the list above. Have them copy Groups 91-93 into their spelling notebook.
Tuesday:	Have students copy Groups 94-96 into their spelling notebook. Do Puzzle 1.
Wednesday:	Have students copy Groups 97-98 into their spelling notebook. Do Puzzle 2.
Thursday:	Have students copy Groups 99-100 into their spelling notebook. Do Puzzle 3.
Friday:	Do Puzzle 4 – without the lesson sheet or spelling notebook.
Friday fun:	Using the homonyms above, write a quatrain (4-line poem).

Assignment Schedule for Two-Year Course

Monday:	Give students the list above. Have them copy Groups 91-92 into their spelling notebook.
Tuesday:	Have students copy Groups 93-94 into their spelling notebook.
Wednesday:	Have students copy Groups 95-96 into their spelling notebook.
Thursday:	Have students copy Groups 97-98 into their spelling notebook.
Friday:	Have students copy Groups 99-100 into their spelling notebook.
Monday:	Do Puzzle 1.
Tuesday:	Do Puzzle 2.
Wednesday:	Do Puzzle 3.
Thursday:	Do Puzzle 4. – without the lesson sheet or spelling notebook.
Friday fun:	Using the homonyms above, write a quatrain (4-line poem).

HOMONYMS 91-100, PUZZLE 1

Use the clues to find the answers in the crossword puzzle.

ACROSS

1 a prophet; one who sees
5 to be ill or sick
6 a unit of weight for gold
7 one who visits another
9 an accomplishment
11 an alcoholic beverage made from grain
12 something owed at a particular time
13 to give up something voluntarily
14 to swarm or abound
15 verb meaning to accomplish something

DOWN

1 to quickly burn the exterior
2 a unit of weight for precious stones
3 a long horizontal pole that dancers use for stretching
4 move the hand repeatedly as a signal
7 to form an opinion without knowing for certain, past tense
8 a long, orange vegetable
9 the body part we walk on
10 a group or band. a side or players
12 moisture that accumulates on the ground over night

HOMONYMS 91-100, PUZZLE 2

Use the clues to find the answers in the word search puzzle. Words can be found horizontally, vertically, or diagonally.

```
E   N   L   L   I   A   Z   H   M   T   C
N   L   E   U   D   T   N   D   A   R   Y
Q   Z   A   C   A   R   A   T   E   Y   F
H   Q   D   N   D   R   T   E   V   W   T
E   C   E   O   R   R   S   E   F   S   J
Y   A   S   T   E   A   M   P   E   M   F
T   R   S   W   B   E   Q   U   W   M   E
E   R   E   A   R   S   G   A   N   R   D
E   O   U   I   A   G   V   P   R   W   H
F   T   G   V   B   E   K   A   R   A   T
G   N   M   E   R   M   B   Z   N   N   B
```

_____ 1. to quickly burn the exterior
_____ 2. an accomplishment
_____ 3. a unit of weight for gold
_____ 4. a long, orange vegetable
_____ 5. to be ill or sick
_____ 6. a group or band. a side or players
_____ 7. to swarm or abound
_____ 8. to prevent someone or something from passing
_____ 9. to give up something voluntarily
_____ 10. cut grass that is used as food for cows and horses
_____ 11. move the hand repeatedly as a signal
_____ 12. an alcoholic beverage made from grain
_____ 13. one who visits another
_____ 14. the body part we walk on
_____ 15. a long horizontal pole that dancers use for stretching
_____ 16. a unit of weight for precious stones
_____ 17. moisture that accumulates on the ground over night
_____ 18. verb meaning to accomplish something
_____ 19. something owed at a particular time
_____ 20. a prophet; one who sees
_____ 21. to form an opinion without knowing for certain, past tense
_____ 22. an interjection to call for a person's attention; a greeting

64

HOMONYMS 91-100, PUZZLE 3

Use the clues to find the answers in the crossword puzzle.

ACROSS

3 a unit of weight for precious stones

4 verb meaning to accomplish something

9 to be ill or sick

10 move the hand repeatedly as a signal

11 to form an opinion without knowing for certain, past tense

13 a long horizontal pole that dancers use for stretching

14 the body part we walk on

16 a long, orange vegetable

17 a group or band. a side or players

DOWN

1 an accomplishment

2 to give up something voluntarily

4 moisture that accumulates on the ground over night

5 a unit of weight for gold

6 an alcoholic beverage made from grain

7 to quickly burn the exterior

8 to swarm or abound

11 one who visits another

12 something owed at a particular time

13 to prevent someone or something from passing

15 cut grass that is used as food for cows and horses

HOMONYMS 91-100, PUZZLE 4

Use the clues to find the answers in the word search puzzle. Words can be found horizontally, vertically, or diagonally.

```
H   A   Y   T   J   K   W   T   T   Y   W
R   T   E   Y   E   A   R   T   A   N   A
Y   E   D   R   V   L   H   H   E   K   I
F   J   R   E   C   X   E   E   F   A   V
M   A   D   V   L   A   T   U   Y   R   E
B   E   T   R   Z   J   R   E   D   A   N
W   R   R   S   H   R   R   R   E   T   L
T   E   A   M   E   O   D   A   O   M   Z
K   W   B   E   P   U   R   E   E   T   L
D   E   S   S   E   U   G   S   N   L   Z
J   H   L   I   A   C   A   R   A   T   A
```

_____ 1. an accomplishment
_____ 2. one who visits another
_____ 3. a unit of weight for gold
_____ 4. a long, orange vegetable
_____ 5. to be ill or sick
_____ 6. the body part we walk on
_____ 7. a group or band. a side or players
_____ 8. to swarm or abound
_____ 9. to give up something voluntarily
_____ 10. cut grass that is used as food for cows and horses
_____ 11. to quickly burn the exterior
_____ 12. move the hand repeatedly as a signal
_____ 13. an alcoholic beverage made from grain
_____ 14. a unit of weight for precious stones
_____ 15. moisture that accumulates on the ground over night
_____ 16. to prevent someone or something from passing
_____ 17. verb meaning to accomplish something
_____ 18. something owed at a particular time
_____ 19. a prophet; one who sees
_____ 20. to form an opinion without knowing for certain, past tense
_____ 21. a long horizontal pole that dancers use for stretching
_____ 22. an interjection to call for a person's attention; a greeting

LESSON 11: HOMONYMS 101 - 110

101.	Leak: Leek:	A slow drip. A garden herb similar to an onion.
102.	Mantel: Mantle:	A shelf over the fireplace. A cloak.
103.	Patience: Patients:	An attitude of being long-suffering. Sick people.
104.	Read: Red:	To decode letters and derive meaning, past tense. A bright color.
105.	Seam: Seem:	The place where two pieces of fabric are sewn together. Appears.
106.	Tear: Tier:	A drop of moisture when one cries. A row, level, or layer.
107.	Walk: Wok:	To move forward at a measured pace. A Chinese cooking pan.
108.	Air: Heir:	Atmosphere, space, sky. Successor, inheritor.
109.	Bases: Basis:	Places of safety (such as, military or baseball bases) The foundation of something.
110.	Caster: Castor:	Wheels on the bottom of furniture. An Indian plant oil with healing properties.

Assignment Schedule for One-Year Course

Monday:	Give students the list above. Have them copy Groups 101-103 into their spelling notebook.
Tuesday:	Have students copy Groups 104-106 into their spelling notebook. Do Puzzle 1.
Wednesday:	Have students copy Groups 107-108 into their spelling notebook. Do Puzzle 2.
Thursday:	Have students copy Groups 109-110 into their spelling notebook. Do Puzzle 3.
Friday:	Do Puzzle 4 – without the lesson sheet or spelling notebook.
Friday fun:	John (or Betty) got sick and needed medical treatment. In a couple of paragraphs, tell the story.

Assignment Schedule for Two-Year Course

Monday:	Give students the list above. Have them copy Groups 101-102 into their spelling notebook.
Tuesday:	Have students copy Groups 103-104 into their spelling notebook.
Wednesday:	Have students copy Groups 105-106 into their spelling notebook.
Thursday:	Have students copy Groups 107-108 into their spelling notebook.
Friday:	Have students copy Groups 109-110 into their spelling notebook.
Monday:	Do Puzzle 1.
Tuesday:	Do Puzzle 2.
Wednesday:	Do Puzzle 3.
Thursday:	Do Puzzle 4. – without the lesson sheet or spelling notebook.
Friday fun:	John (or Betty) got sick and needed medical treatment. In a couple of paragraphs, tell the story.

HOMONYMS 101-110, PUZZLE 1

Use the clues to find the answers in the crossword puzzle.

ACROSS

2 a drop of moisture when one cries
3 appears
6 an attitude of being long-suffering
8 an Indian plant oil with healing
   properties
10 successor, inheritor
11 the foundation of something
12 atmosphere, space, sky
13 the place where two pieces of fabric
   are sewn together
15 a slow drip
16 to move forward at a measured pace
17 a garden herb similar to an onion

DOWN

1 sick people
4 a cloak
5 a bright color
7 a row, level, or layer
8 wheels on the bottom of furniture
9 to decode letters and derive
   meaning, past tense
11 places of safety (such as, military or
   baseball bases)
14 a shelf over the fireplace
16 a Chinese cooking pan

HOMONYMS 101-110, PUZZLE 2

Use the clues to find the answers in the word search puzzle. Words can be found horizontally, vertically, or diagonally.

```
T  R  K  K  R  V  D  W  K  P  R  C  S
L  N  E  V  W  T  H  N  A  R  P  A  E
W  E  R  D  A  M  I  K  E  M  A  S  S
L  N  K  R  L  T  M  E  L  A  T  T  A
R  N  Y  R  K  C  Q  K  R  E  I  O  B
E  Z  M  A  N  T  E  L  P  S  E  R  F
T  X  M  F  B  N  H  A  W  Q  N  K  L
S  R  V  A  S  P  T  O  R  B  C  M  G
A  R  I  I  N  I  K  R  M  H  E  T  T
C  D  S  E  E  T  E  A  R  E  T  T  Z
X  A  E  N  H  V  L  N  S  T  R  I  A
B  T  T  R  X  F  D  E  D  F  M  T  C
K  S  Q  R  X  X  D  A  E  R  N  L  P
```

_____ 1. a bright color
_____ 2. a slow drip
_____ 3. appears
_____ 4. successor, inheritor
_____ 5. a cloak
_____ 6. sick people
_____ 7. to decode letters and derive meaning, past tense
_____ 8. the foundation of something
_____ 9. a Chinese cooking pan
_____ 10. the place where two pieces of fabric are sewn together
_____ 11. a drop of moisture when one cries
_____ 12. a shelf over the fireplace
_____ 13. a row, level, or layer
_____ 14. a garden herb similar to an onion
_____ 15. to move forward at a measured pace
_____ 16. wheels on the bottom of furniture
_____ 17. atmosphere, space, sky
_____ 18. places of safety
_____ 19. an attitude of being long-suffering
_____ 20. an Indian plant oil with healing properties

Made with 1-2-3 Word Search Maker

HOMONYMS 101-110, PUZZLE 3

Use the clues to find the answers in the crossword puzzle.

ACROSS

3 a slow drip
5 an attitude of being long-suffering
7 wheels on the bottom of furniture
11 atmosphere, space, sky
12 a drop of moisture when one cries
14 sick people
16 a Chinese cooking pan
17 a shelf over the fireplace
18 appears

DOWN

1 to move forward at a measured pace
2 a row, level, or layer
3 a garden herb similar to an onion
4 a cloak
6 successor, inheritor
7 an Indian plant oil with healing properties
8 the foundation of something
9 places of safety (such as, military or baseball bases)
10 the place where two pieces of fabric are sewn together
13 to decode letters and derive meaning, past tense
15 a bright color

HOMONYMS 101-110, PUZZLE 4

Use the clues to find the answers in the word search puzzle. Words can be found horizontally, vertically, or diagonally.

```
Y  M  M  M  R  W  W  P  D  V  Z  M
G  A  E  K  M  C  A  S  T  E  R  C
T  E  T  R  S  T  X  K  Z  B  R  M
S  S  J  I  I  R  E  K  S  W  R  T
P  X  S  E  E  E  X  A  E  A  R  P
V  A  N  M  L  R  H  E  S  L  C  A
B  T  Q  K  A  H  J  L  A  K  A  T
S  Z  B  L  N  N  K  M  B  L  S  I
M  A  N  T  E  L  T  E  A  R  T  E
P  H  P  N  D  W  D  L  K  M  O  N
B  N  F  T  O  R  F  V  E  T  R  C
M  C  Y  K  R  I  A  D  A  E  R  E
```

_____ 1. a bright color
_____ 2. a cloak
_____ 3. atmosphere, space, sky
_____ 4. a slow drip
_____ 5. appears
_____ 6. successor, inheritor
_____ 7. the foundation of something
_____ 8. sick people
_____ 9. to decode letters and derive meaning, past tense
_____ 10. a row, level, or layer
_____ 11. a Chinese cooking pan
_____ 12. a drop of moisture when one cries
_____ 13. a shelf over the fireplace
_____ 14. an attitude of being long-suffering
_____ 15. a garden herb similar to an onion
_____ 16. to move forward at a measured pace
_____ 17. wheels on the bottom of furniture
_____ 18. places of safety
_____ 19. an Indian plant oil with healing properties
_____ 20. the place where two pieces of fabric are sewn together

LESSON 12: HOMONYMS 111 - 120

111.	Die: Dye:	To cease to live. To change the color of something.
112.	Find: Fined:	To locate something. To be required to pay a fee, past tense.
113.	Heal: Heel:	To make one better. (Match the "a" with "ail.") The back of the foot.
114.	Lean: Lien:	To bend, tilt. To rest, prop up. Thin or slender. A notice of debt that is placed against property (car or home).
115.	Mare: Mayor:	A female horse. A person who leads/governs a city.
116.	Pause: Paws:	To cause a break in the action. The feet of an animal.
117.	Read: Reed:	To decode letters and derive meaning. A tall, slender grass plant.
118.	Seas: Sees: Seize:	Bodies of water larger than lakes and smaller than oceans. To use the eyes to observe things. To grab something.
119.	Their: There: They're	Possessive pronoun meaning that several people own something. Not here. Contraction of the words *they* and *are*.
120.	Wan: Won:	Pale. To achieve a victory, past tense.

Assignment Schedule for One-Year Course

Monday:	Give students the list above. Have them copy Groups 111-113 into their spelling notebook..
Tuesday:	Have students copy Groups 114-116 into their spelling notebook. Do Puzzle 1.
Wednesday:	Have students copy Groups 117-118 into their spelling notebook. Do Puzzle 2.
Thursday:	Have students copy Groups 119-120 into their spelling notebook. Do Puzzle 3.
Friday:	Do Puzzle 4 – without the lesson sheet or spelling notebook.
Friday fun:	The mayor is concerned about the treatment of animals in his town. Write about the things he doesn't like and make suggestions to improve the lives of dogs and cats. Remember to use as many of these homonyms as you can.

Assignment Schedule for Two-Year Course

Monday:	Give students the list above. Have them copy Groups 111-112 into their spelling notebook.
Tuesday:	Have students copy Groups 113-114 into their spelling notebook.
Wednesday:	Have students copy Groups 115-116 into their spelling notebook.
Thursday:	Have students copy Groups 117-118 into their spelling notebook.
Friday:	Have students copy Groups 119-120 into their spelling notebook.
Monday:	Do Puzzle 1.
Tuesday:	Do Puzzle 2.
Wednesday:	Do Puzzle 3.
Thursday:	Do Puzzle 4. – without the lesson sheet or spelling notebook.
Friday fun:	The mayor is concerned about the treatment of animals in his town. Write about the things he doesn't like and make suggestions to improve the lives of dogs and cats. Remember to use as many of these homonyms as you can.

HOMONYMS 111-120, PUZZLE 1

Use the clues to find the answers in the crossword puzzle.

ACROSS

3 bodies of water larger than lakes and smaller than oceans
4 contraction of the words they and are
5 not here
6 the feet of an animal
7 a notice of debt that is placed against property (car or home)
8 to decode letters and derive meaning
9 a person who leads/governs a city
11 the back of the foot
13 to be required to pay a fee, past tense
15 to achieve a victory, past tense
16 to bend, tilt; to rest, prop up; thin or slender

DOWN

1 to use the eyes to observe things
2 to make one better
3 to grab something
5 possessive pronoun meaning that several people own something
6 to cause a break in the action
8 a tall, slender grass plant
9 a female horse
10 to locate something
12 to cease to live
14 to change the color of something
15 pale

HOMONYMS 111-120, PUZZLE 2

Use the clues to find the answers in the word search puzzle. Words can be found horizontally, vertically, or diagonally.

```
N   A   E   L   P   R   D   W   E   P   J   B
H   F   V   R   T   A   R   O   I   R   G   E
E   Z   F   N   R   N   W   N   D   E   Y   R
A   L   K   I   E   C   J   S   Y   R   O   A
L   H   E   M   N   I   V   D   E   Y   Y   M
G   H   G   D   F   E   L   E   A   N   G   E
T   F   S   B   N   M   D   M   N   K   E   R
R   P   P   E   N   P   A   U   S   E   Z   '
E   B   K   R   E   H   S   A   E   S   I   Y
A   W   F   L   E   S   K   J   X   N   E   E
D   R   A   E   T   H   F   I   N   D   S   H
W   D   L   N   F   T   H   E   R   E   X   T
```

_____ 1. to locate something
_____ 2. a tall, slender grass plant
_____ 3. to grab something
_____ 4. to cease to live
_____ 5. not here
_____ 6. the feet of an animal
_____ 7. pale
_____ 8. to be required to pay a fee, past tense
_____ 9. to make one better
_____ 10. to use the eyes to observe things
_____ 11. a female horse
_____ 12. contraction of the words _they_ and _are_
_____ 13. the back of the foot
_____ 14. a notice of debt that is placed against property (car or home)
_____ 15. a person who leads/governs a city
_____ 16. to cause a break in the action
_____ 17. to bend, tilt; to rest, prop up; thin or slender
_____ 18. to decode letters and derive meaning
_____ 19. to change the color of something
_____ 20. bodies of water larger than lakes and smaller than oceans
_____ 21. possessive pronoun meaning that several people own something
_____ 22. to achieve a victory, past tense

HOMONYMS 111-120, PUZZLE 3

Use the clues to find the answers in the crossword puzzle.

ACROSS

1 to achieve a victory, past tense
3 a tall, slender grass plant
5 to locate something
6 to decode letters and derive meaning
8 to bend, tilt; to rest, prop up; thin or slender
9 not here
12 contraction of the words they and are
13 to change the color of something
14 to cause a break in the action
17 a person who leads/governs a city
18 the back of the foot
19 bodies of water larger than lakes and smaller than oceans

DOWN

1 pale
2 a female horse
4 to cease to live
5 to be required to pay a fee, past tense
7 possessive pronoun meaning that several people own something
8 a notice of debt that is placed against property (car or home)
10 to make one better
11 to grab something
15 to use the eyes to observe things
16 the feet of an animal

HOMONYMS 111-120, PUZZLE 4

Use the clues to find the answers in the word search puzzle. Words can be found horizontally, vertically, or diagonally.

```
W  K  J  P  J  R  X  R  Y  W  T  M
F  I  N  D  I  P  A  U  S  E  R  H
R  L  Q  E  C  P  R  P  N  Q  E  N
E  P  H  H  G  E  E  W  L  E  F  M
A  T  G  F  E  N  R  O  L  E  R  E
D  H  E  D  I  T  A  N  J  I  N  R
S  N  Z  P  J  N  M  N  H  D  R  '
J  E  I  C  A  V  E  R  E  R  T  Y
N  A  E  L  L  W  O  D  A  I  K  E
W  Y  S  S  T  Y  S  Y  L  F  L  H
D  A  N  T  A  W  T  H  E  R  E  T
Q  P  N  M  D  S  A  E  S  C  N  N
```

_____ 1. pale
_____ 2. not here
_____ 3. to locate something
_____ 4. to change the color of something
_____ 5. to be required to pay a fee, past tense
_____ 6. a tall, slender grass plant
_____ 7. to grab something
_____ 8. to cease to live
_____ 9. the feet of an animal
_____ 10. a person who leads/governs a city
_____ 11. to make one better
_____ 12. to achieve a victory, past tense
_____ 13. to use the eyes to observe things
_____ 14. a female horse
_____ 15. contraction of the words *they* and *are*
_____ 16. the back of the foot
_____ 17. a notice of debt that is placed against property (car or home)
_____ 18. to cause a break in the action
_____ 19. to bend, tilt; to rest, prop up; thin or slender
_____ 20. to decode letters and derive meaning
_____ 21. bodies of water larger than lakes and smaller than oceans
_____ 22. possessive pronoun meaning that several people own something

LESSON 13: HOMONYMS 121 - 130

121.	Aisle: I'll: Isle:	A walkway or passageway. Contraction of *I* and *will*. A small island.
122.	Be: Bea: Bee:	To exist. A woman's name, short for Beatrice or Beatrix. An insect that makes honey.
123.	Caught: Cot:	To catch, past tense. A small bed, often transportable.
124.	Died: Dyed:	To cease to live, past tense. To change the color of something, past tense.
125.	Flair: Flare:	Flamboyant use of a talent or thing. A bright light used to signal distress.
126.	Hear: Here:	A sense that involves the ear. At this spot.
127.	Led: Lead:	To be the front person escorting another, past tense. A metal; formerly, the center of a pencil.
128.	Marry: Mary Merry:	To join in matrimony. A woman's name. Happy.
129.	Pea: Pee:	A small, round vegetable. The 16th letter of the alphabet.
130.	Real: Reel:	True. A spool on which things are wound.

Assignment Schedule for One-Year Course

Monday:	Give students the list above. Have them copy Groups 121-123 into their spelling notebook.
Tuesday:	Have students copy Groups 124-126 into their spelling notebook. Do Puzzle 1.
Wednesday:	Have students copy Groups 127-128 into their spelling notebook. Do Puzzle 2.
Thursday:	Have students copy Groups 129-130 into their spelling notebook. Do Puzzle 3.
Friday:	Do Puzzle 4 – without the lesson sheet or spelling notebook.
Friday fun:	Oh, no! You're stranded on a desert isle. Tell about your life there and your hopes for rescue. Use as many of the homonyms as you can.

Assignment Schedule for Two-Year Course

Monday:	Give students the list above. Have them copy Groups 121-122 into their spelling notebook.
Tuesday:	Have students copy Groups 123-124 into their spelling notebook.
Wednesday:	Have students copy Groups 125-126 into their spelling notebook.
Thursday:	Have students copy Groups 127-128 into their spelling notebook.
Friday:	Have students copy Groups 129-130 into their spelling notebook.
Monday:	Do Puzzle 1.
Tuesday:	Do Puzzle 2.
Wednesday:	Do Puzzle 3.
Thursday:	Do Puzzle 4. – without the lesson sheet or spelling notebook.
Friday fun:	Oh, no! You're stranded on a desert isle. Tell about your life there and your hopes for rescue. Use as many of the homonyms as you can.

HOMONYMS 121-130, PUZZLE 1

Use the clues to find the answers in the crossword puzzle.

ACROSS

1 a woman's name, short for Beatrice or Beatrix
3 to be the front person escorting another, past tense
6 a small, round vegetable
8 true
10 to cease to live, past tense
11 a walkway or passageway
12 contraction of i and will
13 to join in matrimony
14 to exist
15 at this spot
16 to catch, past tense

DOWN

1 an insect that makes honey
2 a bright light used to signal distress
3 a metal; formerly, the center of a pencil
4 to change the color of something, past tense
5 flamboyant use of a talent or thing
6 the 16th letter of the alphabet
7 a spool on which things are wound
9 a woman's name
12 a small island
13 happy
15 a sense that involves the ear

HOMONYMS 121-130, PUZZLE 2

Use the clues to find the answers in the word search puzzle. Words can be found horizontally, vertically, or diagonally.

```
D  Y  D  E  L  T  H  G  U  A  C
E  R  T  N  D  B  M  A  R  R  Y
I  A  B  O  E  T  Y  I  S  L  E
D  M  D  E  C  R  F  R  P  M  K
H  E  D  A  R  M  D  L  E  E  R
E  L  R  E  E  L  B  A  Z  A  A
A  S  M  R  Y  L  M  E  K  R  M
R  I  E  D  '  M  B  A  P  H  E
M  A  D  I  G  M  Z  L  E  Y  P
L  Q  K  C  D  M  D  R  V  K  E
F  L  A  I  R  L  E  V  X  Q  E
```

_____ 1. to exist
_____ 2. contraction of *i* and *will*
_____ 3. an insect that makes honey
_____ 4. to catch, past tense
_____ 5. at this spot
_____ 6. a small bed, often transportable
_____ 7. to change the color of something, past tense
_____ 8. a small island
_____ 9. flamboyant use of a talent or thing
_____ 10. true
_____ 11. a bright light used to signal distress
_____ 12. a sense that involves the ear
_____ 13. to be the front person escorting another, past tense
_____ 14. a small, round vegetable
_____ 15. a woman's name
_____ 16. to cease to live, past tense
_____ 17. a metal; formerly, the center of a pencil
_____ 18. to join in matrimony
_____ 19. a woman's name, short for Beatrice or Beatrix
_____ 20. a walkway or passageway
_____ 21. happy
_____ 22. the 16th letter of the alphabet
_____ 23. a spool on which things are wound

Made with Crossword Weaver

HOMONYMS 121-130, PUZZLE 3

Use the clues to find the answers in the crossword puzzle.

ACROSS

3 a sense that involves the ear
5 to catch, past tense
7 a bright light used to signal distress
8 a woman's name, short for Beatrice or Beatrix
9 a small, round vegetable
11 contraction of i and will
13 happy
15 a small island
16 to join in matrimony
17 to change the color of something, past tense
18 to be the front person escorting another, past tense
19 an insect that makes honey

DOWN

1 a spool on which things are wound
2 a small bed, often transportable
4 to exist
6 at this spot
7 flamboyant use of a talent or thing
9 the 16th letter of the alphabet
10 a walkway or passageway
12 a metal; formerly, the center of a pencil
13 a woman's name
14 true
17 to cease to live, past tense

HOMONYMS 121-130, PUZZLE 4

Use the clues to find the answers in the word search puzzle. Words can be found horizontally, vertically, or diagonally.

```
Q  R  B  D  I  S  L  E  V  A
L  X  E  E  A  D  E  L  E  B
F  Y  A  I  L  E  P  P  E  L
D  L  B  D  E  L  L  E  L  H
T  T  A  E  E  S  W  '  E  D
Y  R  O  R  R  I  I  R  H  Q
R  E  T  C  E  A  E  N  E  R
R  A  W  M  T  H  G  U  A  C
A  L  F  L  A  I  R  M  R  N
M  M  A  R  Y  Y  R  R  E  M
```

_____ 1. contraction of *i* and *will*
_____ 2. true
_____ 3. an insect that makes honey
_____ 4. a woman's name
_____ 5. to catch, past tense
_____ 6. at this spot
_____ 7. happy
_____ 8. a small bed, often transportable
_____ 9. to change the color of something, past tense
_____ 10. a small island
_____ 11. a sense that involves the ear
_____ 12. a woman's name, short for Beatrice or Beatrix
_____ 13. to be the front person escorting another, past tense
_____ 14. to exist
_____ 15. a small, round vegetable
_____ 16. to cease to live, past tense
_____ 17. flamboyant use of a talent or thing
_____ 18. a metal; formerly, the center of a pencil
_____ 19. to join in matrimony
_____ 20. a bright light used to signal distress
_____ 21. a walkway or passageway
_____ 22. the 16th letter of the alphabet
_____ 23. a spool on which things are wound

LESSON 14: HOMONYMS 131 - 140

131.	Sew: So: Sow:	Use needle and thread to join two pieces of fabric. A coordinating conjunction used to join two simple sentences. A subordinating conjunction meaning *in order to.* To plant seeds.
132.	Threw: Through:	To throw. (Match the "e" with elbow.) Preposition meaning to pass between.
133.	War: Wore:	A conflict. To put on (clothes), past tense.
134.	All: Awl:	Each and every one. A large sewing needle, often used for punching holes in leather.
135.	Beach: Beech:	The sandy place between land and sea. A type of tree used in making furniture; a shrub.
136.	Cawed: Cod:	The sound made by a crow, past tense. A type of fish typically found in northern waters.
137.	Doe: Dough:	A female deer. Money.
138.	Flea: Flee:	An insect that lives on mammals. To run away.
139.	Heard: Herd:	To sense something with the ear, past tense. A large group of one type of animals.
140.	Lent: Lint:	A period of sacrifice in the Christian faith. Loose cotton that collects in the corners of pockets.

Assignment Schedule for One-Year Course

Monday:	Give students the list above. Have them copy Groups 131-133 into their spelling notebook.
Tuesday:	Have students copy Groups 134-136 into their spelling notebook. Do Puzzle 1.
Wednesday:	Have students copy Groups 137-138 into their spelling notebook. Do Puzzle 2.
Thursday:	Have students copy Groups 139-140 into their spelling notebook. Do Puzzle 3.
Friday:	Do Puzzle 4 – without the lesson sheet or spelling notebook.
Friday fun:	It's time for another limerick. Write a limerick using some of the homonyms above.

Assignment Schedule for Two-Year Course

Monday:	Give students the list above. Have them copy Groups 131-132 into their spelling notebook.
Tuesday:	Have students copy Groups 133-134 into their spelling notebook.
Wednesday:	Have students copy Groups 135-136 into their spelling notebook.
Thursday:	Have students copy Groups 137-138 into their spelling notebook.
Friday:	Have students copy Groups 139-140 into their spelling notebook.
Monday:	Do Puzzle 1.
Tuesday:	Do Puzzle 2.
Wednesday:	Do Puzzle 3.
Thursday:	Do Puzzle 4. – without the lesson sheet or spelling notebook.
Friday fun:	It's time for another limerick. Write a limerick using some of the homonyms above.

HOMONYMS 131-140, PUZZLE 1

Use the clues to find the answers in the crossword puzzle.

ACROSS

1 to run away
3 a type of tree used in making furniture; a shrub
6 use needle and thread to join two pieces of fabric
7 each and every one
9 a conflict
10 preposition meaning to pass between
11 money
14 a coordinating conjunction used to join two simple sentences
15 the sound made by a crow, past tense
17 a large group of one type of animals
18 a period of sacrifice in the Christian faith

DOWN

1 an insect that lives on mammals
2 the sandy place between land and sea
4 to sense something with the ear, past tense
5 a large sewing needle used for punching holes in leather
8 to plant seeds
10 to throw
12 to put on (clothes), past tense
13 loose cotton that collects in the corners of pockets
15 a type of fish typically found in northern waters
16 a female deer

HOMONYMS 131-140, PUZZLE 2

Use the clues to find the answers in the word search puzzle. Words can be found horizontally, vertically, or diagonally.

```
C  P  Z  A  C  E  R  O  W  W
O  C  T  N  E  L  N  H  B  E
D  T  A  H  D  L  C  F  T  S
C  K  M  W  R  A  F  Z  H  D
C  M  D  B  E  E  C  H  R  L
Q  O  W  B  H  D  W  A  O  E
E  A  N  L  L  Y  E  S  U  E
R  T  N  I  L  H  Q  L  G  L
P  T  S  O  W  A  V  W  H  F
K  P  H  G  U  O  D  A  M  Z
```

_____ 1. use needle and thread to join two pieces of fabric
_____ 2. a conjunction used to join two simple sentences
_____ 3. money
_____ 4. to throw
_____ 5. a type of fish typically found in northern waters
_____ 6. a conflict
_____ 7. a type of tree used in making furniture; a shrub
_____ 8. an insect that lives on mammals
_____ 9. each and every one
_____ 10. the sandy place between land and sea
_____ 11. to plant seeds
_____ 12. the sound made by a crow, past tense
_____ 13. a female deer
_____ 14. a period of sacrifice in the Christian faith
_____ 15. to run away
_____ 16. to sense something with the ear, past tense
_____ 17. a large sewing needle used for punching holes in leather
_____ 18. to put on (clothes), past tense
_____ 19. a large group of one type of animals
_____ 20. preposition meaning to pass between
_____ 21. loose cotton that collects in the corners of pockets

88   Made with 1-2-3 Word Search Maker

HOMONYMS 131-140, PUZZLE 3

Use the clues to find the answers in the crossword puzzle.

ACROSS

3 money
5 the sandy place between land and sea
7 to run away
8 a conflict
10 to put on (clothes), past tense
12 each and every one
14 a period of sacrifice in the Christian faith
15 to sense something with the ear, past tense
17 a type of fish typically found in northern waters
19 preposition meaning to pass between

DOWN

1 a coordinating conjunction used to join two simple sentences
2 to throw
4 use needle and thread to join two pieces of fabric
6 the sound made by a crow, past tense
7 an insect that lives on mammals
9 a large sewing needle used for punching holes in leather
11 a type of tree used in making furniture; a shrub
13 loose cotton that collects in the corners of pockets
16 to plant seeds
18 a female deer
20 a large group of one type of animals

Made with Crossword Weaver

HOMONYMS 131-140, PUZZLE 4

Use the clues to find the answers in the word search puzzle. Words can be found horizontally, vertically, or diagonally.

```
H E R D H B E E C H L
T Y R C V F W L T L I
J K A K X A J W H R N
Q E N E R O W A R H T
B M P W S O W C O T C
T T D E G V D D U L O
C H Y S A R O B G E D
T A R L A E L W H E N
H F W E E B L L G L F
D D H E W N Z F A F O
H G U O D L T R T S Y
```

_____ 1. a conjunction used to join two simple sentences
_____ 2. each and every one
_____ 3. money
_____ 4. to throw
_____ 5. a conflict
_____ 6. a type of tree used in making furniture; a shrub
_____ 7. an insect that lives on mammals
_____ 8. to put on (clothes), past tense
_____ 9. the sandy place between land and sea
_____ 10. to plant seeds
_____ 11. the sound made by a crow, past tense
_____ 12. a female deer
_____ 13. preposition meaning to pass between
_____ 14. a period of sacrifice in the Christian faith
_____ 15. use needle and thread to join two pieces of fabric
_____ 16. to run away
_____ 17. to sense something with the ear, past tense
_____ 18. a large sewing needle used for punching holes in leather
_____ 19. a large group of one type of animals
_____ 20. a type of fish typically found in northern waters
_____ 21. loose cotton that collects in the corners of pockets

LESSON 15: HOMONYMS 141 - 150

141.	Meat:	Animal flesh.
	Meet:	To make someone's acquaintance.
142.	Peace:	Calm.
	Piece:	A part of something.
143.	Reck:	An old term for worry or care.
	Wreck:	A ruined hulk
144.	Shear:	To cut off, shave, clip, or trim.
	Sheer:	Adjective meaning pure/complete or steep/vertical.
145.	Thyme:	A seasoning.
	Time:	Minute or hour. System of distinguishing events.
146.	Ware:	Product for sale.
	Wear:	To put on.
	Where:	A place.
147.	Allowed:	To permit, past tense.
	Aloud:	Spoken so someone can hear.
148.	Beat:	To strike something; to win.
	Beet:	A red vegetable with a high sugar content.
149.	Cede:	To yield or concede.
	Seed:	Kernel used to start a new plant; verb meaning to plant/sow.
150.	Does:	A form of the verb *do*.
	Dose:	A prescribed amount or quantity. *Near homonym; included because* does *is frequently misspelled.*

Assignment Schedule for One-Year Course

Monday:	Give students the list above. Have them copy Groups 141-143 into their spelling notebook.
Tuesday:	Have students copy Groups 144-146 into their spelling notebook. Do Puzzle 1.
Wednesday:	Have students copy Groups 147-148 into their spelling notebook. Do Puzzle 2.
Thursday:	Have students copy Groups 149-150 into their spelling notebook. Do Puzzle 3.
Friday:	Do Puzzle 4 – without the lesson sheet or spelling notebook.
Friday fun:	Write a short story (2-4 paragraphs) on a trip to the grocery store. Use as many of these homonyms as you can..

Assignment Schedule for Two-Year Course

Monday:	Give students the list above. Have them copy Groups 141-142 into their spelling notebook.
Tuesday:	Have students copy Groups 143-144 into their spelling notebook.
Wednesday:	Have students copy Groups 145-146 into their spelling notebook.
Thursday:	Have students copy Groups 147-148 into their spelling notebook.
Friday:	Have students copy Groups 149-150 into their spelling notebook.
Monday:	Do Puzzle 1.
Tuesday:	Do Puzzle 2.
Wednesday:	Do Puzzle 3.
Thursday:	Do Puzzle 4. – without the lesson sheet or spelling notebook.
Friday fun:	Write a short story (2-4 paragraphs) on a trip to the grocery store. Use as many of these homonyms as you can..

HOMONYMS 141-150, PUZZLE 1

Use the clues to find the answers in the crossword puzzle.

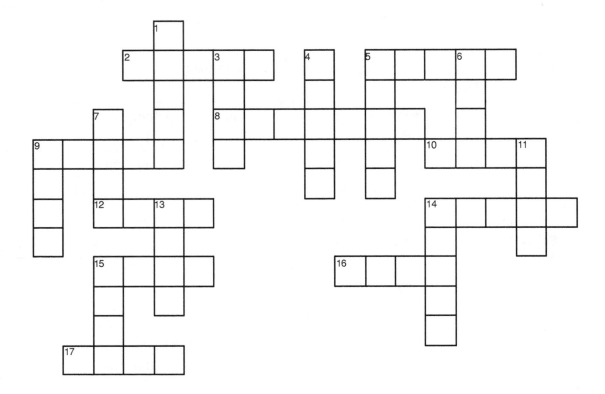

ACROSS

2 a seasoning
5 a ruined hulk
8 to permit, past tense
9 to cut off, shave, clip, or trim
10 to put on
12 minute or hour. system of distinguishing events
14 calm
15 a form of the verb do
16 product for sale
17 to strike something; to win

DOWN

1 adjective meaning pure/complete or steep/vertical
3 animal flesh
4 spoken so someone can hear
5 a place
6 to yield or concede
7 a red vegetable with a high sugar content
9 kernel used to start a new plant
11 an old term for worry or care
13 to make someone's acquaintance
14 a part of something
15 a prescribed amount or quantity

HOMONYMS 141-150, PUZZLE 2

Use the clues to find the answers in the word search puzzle. Words can be found horizontally, vertically, or diagonally.

```
Y  N  T  R  B  K  T  W  H  D  E
F  V  P  E  E  E  T  W  E  M  Q
C  M  A  I  E  E  R  E  I  A  W
F  T  W  M  E  E  H  T  E  M  R
W  A  R  E  C  C  T  S  M  B  M
L  M  T  K  R  D  E  B  Y  W  G
P  E  A  C  E  D  M  T  H  L  W
E  V  R  E  C  L  O  A  T  T  H
D  O  S  E  K  R  A  E  H  S  E
E  D  U  O  L  A  F  M  S  Q  R
C  T  F  D  E  W  O  L  L  A  E
```

_____ 1. calm
_____ 2. to make someone's acquaintance
_____ 3. a place
_____ 4. a part of something
_____ 5. a ruined hulk
_____ 6. to strike something; to win
_____ 7. to yield or concede
_____ 8. animal flesh
_____ 9. to cut off, shave, clip, or trim
_____ 10. a form of the verb *do*
_____ 11. a seasoning
_____ 12. product for sale
_____ 13. to permit, past tense
_____ 14. an old term for worry or care
_____ 15. spoken so someone can hear
_____ 16. a red vegetable with a high sugar content
_____ 17. minute or hour. system of distinguishing events
_____ 18. kernel used to start a new plant
_____ 19. adjective meaning pure/complete or steep/vertical
_____ 20. to put on
_____ 21. a prescribed amount or quantity

HOMONYMS 141-150, PUZZLE 3

Use the clues to find the answers in the crossword puzzle.

ACROSS

1 a red vegetable with a high sugar content
4 to make someone's acquaintance
5 animal flesh
8 kernel used to start a new plant
10 to cut off, shave, clip, or trim
13 product for sale
15 a prescribed amount or quantity
16 to yield or concede
17 a form of the verb do
18 a ruined hulk
19 to permit, past tense

DOWN

1 to strike something; to win
2 a seasoning
3 a place
6 minute or hour. system of distinguishing events
7 to put on
9 calm
10 adjective meaning pure/complete or steep/vertical
11 spoken so someone can hear
12 an old term for worry or care
14 a part of something

HOMONYMS 141-150, PUZZLE 4

Use the clues to find the answers in the word search puzzle. Words can be found horizontally, vertically, or diagonally.

```
W  T  D  S  E  E  D  T  V  T  M
H  E  R  O  L  L  P  N  A  A  Z
E  E  R  A  E  H  S  I  F  E  C
R  B  N  X  T  S  X  K  E  M  B
E  E  R  E  Z  W  A  R  E  C  W
L  L  E  P  E  A  C  E  E  R  E
F  M  C  H  A  W  E  D  E  E  K
L  N  K  L  S  M  E  C  J  M  D
M  F  O  C  I  C  K  A  R  Y  O
T  U  V  T  Z  N  M  M  R  H  S
D  X  D  E  W  O  L  L  A  T  E
```

_____ 1. to cut off, shave, clip, or trim
_____ 2. to make someone's acquaintance
_____ 3. a place
_____ 4. spoken so someone can hear
_____ 5. a part of something
_____ 6. a ruined hulk
_____ 7. a seasoning
_____ 8. to yield or concede
_____ 9. animal flesh
_____ 10. kernel used to start a new plant
_____ 11. a form of the verb *do*
_____ 12. product for sale
_____ 13. to permit, past tense
_____ 14. to strike something; to win
_____ 15. to put on
_____ 16. an old term for worry or care
_____ 17. a red vegetable with a high sugar content
_____ 18. minute or hour. system of distinguishing events
_____ 19. calm
_____ 20. adjective meaning pure/complete or steep/vertical
_____ 21. a prescribed amount or quantity

LESSON 16: HOMONYMS 151 - 160

151.	Fleas: Flees: Fleece:	Insects that live on mammals. Runs away. The hair on sheep that is spun into wool. To cheat or swindle.
152.	Hi: High:	An interjection; a greeting. Elevated. Opposite of low.
153.	Lentil: Lintel:	Edible seed, often thought of as a bean. The part of a door frame over the door.
154.	Medal: Meddle: Metal:	An award for doing something important. To involve oneself in someone else's affairs. A strong, natural substance like iron or steel.
155.	Peak: Peek: Pique:	The top of something. (The "a" resembles a mountain top.) To take a quick look. (The two "Es" are for "eyes.") A bit of annoyance or anger. Interest/attract.
156.	Reek: Wreak:	To stink. To avenge.
157.	Shone: Shown:	To shine, past tense. To show or display, participle.
158.	Tide: Tied:	The ebb and flow of salt water. To join with a knot, past tense.
159.	Way: Weigh:	A road or path. To determine the size or mass.
160.	Ate: Eight:	To consume, specifically food. Past tense. The number between 7 and 9.

Assignment Schedule for One-Year Course

Monday:	Give students the list above. Have them copy Groups 151-153 into their spelling notebook.
Tuesday:	Have students copy Groups 154-156 into their spelling notebook. Do Puzzle 1.
Wednesday:	Have students copy Groups 157-158 into their spelling notebook. Do Puzzle 2.
Thursday:	Have students copy Groups 159-160 into their spelling notebook. Do Puzzle 3.
Friday:	Do Puzzle 4 – without the lesson sheet or spelling notebook.
Friday fun:	The flea circus is in town! Using these homonyms, write a story about a flea circus.

Assignment Schedule for Two-Year Course

Monday:	Give students the list above. Have them copy Groups 151-152 into their spelling notebook.
Tuesday:	Have students copy Groups 153-154 into their spelling notebook.
Wednesday:	Have students copy Groups 155-156 into their spelling notebook.
Thursday:	Have students copy Groups 157-158 into their spelling notebook.
Friday:	Have students copy Groups 159-160 into their spelling notebook.
Monday:	Do Puzzle 1.
Tuesday:	Do Puzzle 2.
Wednesday:	Do Puzzle 3.
Thursday:	Do Puzzle 4. – without the lesson sheet or spelling notebook.
Friday fun:	The flea circus is in town! Using these homonyms, write a story about a flea circus.

HOMONYMS 151-160, PUZZLE 1

Use the clues to find the answers in the crossword puzzle.

ACROSS

2 to show or display, participle
3 to determine the size or mass
5 the part of a door frame over the door
8 a strong, natural substance like iron or steel
9 the number between 7 and 9
11 runs away
13 to join with a knot, past tense
15 to avenge
16 an award for doing something important
17 to consume, specifically food. past tense
18 to take a quick look

DOWN

1 to stink
2 to shine, past tense
4 the hair on sheep that is spun into wool. to cheat or swindle
5 edible seed, often thought of as a bean
6 elevated. opposite of low
7 to involve oneself in someone else's affairs
10 an interjection; a greeting
11 insects that live on mammals
12 a bit of annoyance or anger
13 the ebb and flow of salt water
14 the top of something
15 a road or path

HOMONYMS 151-160, PUZZLE 2

Use the clues to find the answers in the word search puzzle. Words can be found horizontally, vertically, or diagonally.

```
Z  F  L  E  E  C  E  R  S  G  R  H
G  F  A  R  T  L  E  E  W  V  L  Y
N  T  N  T  A  E  E  H  E  W  Q  R
E  G  L  T  K  L  Q  I  I  N  A  R
L  N  E  A  F  P  L  G  G  W  J  Y
D  M  B  M  D  E  E  H  H  O  H  J
D  T  L  E  N  E  D  E  R  H  H  M
E  H  I  T  H  S  M  I  K  S  P  I
M  T  I  G  Q  A  L  E  T  N  I  L
C  L  J  K  A  E  R  W  X  T  Q  K
T  H  G  I  E  L  L  V  M  D  U  M
M  P  E  A  K  F  S  H  O  N  E  N
```

_____ 1. runs away
_____ 2. an interjection; a greeting
_____ 3. edible seed, often thought of as a bean
_____ 4. to stink
_____ 5. a bit of annoyance or anger
_____ 6. an award for doing something important
_____ 7. the ebb and flow of salt water
_____ 8. insects that live on mammals
_____ 9. to shine, past tense
_____ 10. a strong, natural substance like iron or steel
_____ 11. a road or path
_____ 12. the top of something
_____ 13. elevated. opposite of low
_____ 14. to take a quick look
_____ 15. the part of a door frame over the door
_____ 16. to avenge
_____ 17. to consume, specifically food. past tense
_____ 18. to show or display, participle
_____ 19. to join with a knot, past tense
_____ 20. to determine the size or mass
_____ 21. the number between 7 and 9
_____ 22. to involve oneself in someone else's affairs
_____ 23. the hair on sheep that is spun into wool.

100   Made with 1-2-3 Word Search Maker

HOMONYMS 151-160, PUZZLE 3

Use the clues to find the answers in the crossword puzzle.

ACROSS

4 a bit of annoyance or anger
6 to determine the size or mass
7 insects that live on mammals
8 to avenge
11 edible seed, often thought of as a bean
13 the top of something
14 to involve oneself in someone else's affairs
15 the number between 7 and 9
17 to join with a knot, past tense
18 to shine, past tense
19 runs away

DOWN

1 an interjection; a greeting
2 a strong, natural substance like iron or steel
3 to consume, specifically food. past tense
5 to show or display, participle
6 a road or path
7 the hair on sheep that is spun into wool. to cheat or swindle
9 to stink
10 the ebb and flow of salt water
12 the part of a door frame over the door
13 to take a quick look
14 an award for doing something important
16 elevated. opposite of low

HOMONYMS 151-160, PUZZLE 4

Use the clues to find the answers in the word search puzzle. Words can be found horizontally, vertically, or diagonally.

```
J  Q  K  P  D  N  R  F  P  X  C  C
E  H  G  I  E  W  M  M  I  M  S  E
I  P  E  A  K  E  L  N  Q  Y  A  L
G  Z  P  Y  N  A  K  R  U  K  E  D
H  L  L  E  T  N  I  L  E  K  L  D
T  L  A  E  S  H  O  W  N  E  F  E
N  V  M  D  N  M  R  P  N  Z  T  M
S  H  O  N  E  E  B  T  S  A  C  Y
E  H  R  H  E  M  I  E  D  N  Q  W
D  I  H  K  F  L  E  E  C  E  A  L
I  G  Z  I  K  L  N  W  C  Y  I  Y
T  H  N  Q  F  K  A  E  R  W  X  T
```

_____ 1. runs away
_____ 2. to avenge
_____ 3. an interjection; a greeting
_____ 4. a road or path
_____ 5. to stink
_____ 6. a bit of annoyance or anger
_____ 7. an award for doing something important
_____ 8. the ebb and flow of salt water
_____ 9. insects that live on mammals
_____ 10. to shine, past tense
_____ 11. edible seed, often thought of as a bean
_____ 12. to involve oneself in someone else's affairs
_____ 13. a strong, natural substance like iron or steel
_____ 14. to join with a knot, past tense
_____ 15. the top of something
_____ 16. the number between 7 and 9
_____ 17. elevated. opposite of low
_____ 18. to take a quick look
_____ 19. to consume, specifically food. past tense
_____ 20. to show or display, participle
_____ 21. to determine the size or mass
_____ 22. the part of a door frame over the door
_____ 23. the hair on sheep that is spun into wool

LESSON 17: HOMONYMS 161 - 170

161.	Beau: Bow:	French for a boyfriend. A tied ribbon.
162.	Ceiling: Sealing:	The upper surface of a room. To seal or close something.
163.	Does: Doze:	2 or more female deer. To sleep lightly.
164.	Flew: Flu: Flue:	To propel through the air, past tense. Short form of "influenza," an upper respiratory illness. Tube or pipe used to convey heat or smoke outside. [Part of the chimney.]
165.	Him: Hymn:	Personal pronoun referring to a male. A song of praise.
166.	Lessen: Lesson:	To decrease. A concept that is taught.
167.	Mind: Mined:	The body part where our thoughts and memory reside. To obey. To dig in the earth, past tense.
168.	Peal Peel:	To ring out. To remove the exterior of something. Skin, rind, or covering.
169.	Residence: Residents:	A house. People who live in a home or community.
170.	Sighs: Size:	Breaths that are long and loud. How much something measures.

Assignment Schedule for One-Year Course

Monday:	Give students the list above. Have them copy Groups 161-163 into their spelling notebook.
Tuesday:	Have students copy Groups 164-166 into their spelling notebook. Do Puzzle 1.
Wednesday:	Have students copy Groups 167-168 into their spelling notebook. Do Puzzle 2.
Thursday:	Have students copy Groups 169-170 into their spelling notebook. Do Puzzle 3.
Friday:	Do Puzzle 4 – without the lesson sheet or spelling notebook.
Friday fun:	The words in this list lend themselves to a poem or paragraph about a church.

Assignment Schedule for Two-Year Course

Monday:	Give students the list above. Have them copy Groups 161-162 into their spelling notebook.
Tuesday:	Have students copy Groups 163-164 into their spelling notebook.
Wednesday:	Have students copy Groups 165-166 into their spelling notebook.
Thursday:	Have students copy Groups 167-168 into their spelling notebook.
Friday:	Have students copy Groups 169-170 into their spelling notebook.
Monday:	Do Puzzle 1.
Tuesday:	Do Puzzle 2.
Wednesday:	Do Puzzle 3.
Thursday:	Do Puzzle 4. – without the lesson sheet or spelling notebook.
Friday fun:	The words in this list lend themselves to a poem or paragraph about a church.

HOMONYMS 161-170, PUZZLE 1

Use the clues to find the answers in the crossword puzzle.

ACROSS

4 tube or pipe used to convey heat or smoke outside
7 a tied ribbon
8 people who live in a home or community
9 how much something measures
11 to sleep lightly
14 the body part where our thoughts and memory reside
15 to remove the exterior of something
17 a song of praise
18 breaths that are long and loud
19 to seal or close something

DOWN

1 a concept that is taught
2 2 or more female deer
3 to propel through the air, past tense
5 to decrease
6 to dig in the earth, past tense
7 French for a boyfriend
10 a house
12 the upper surface of a room
13 short form of "influenza," an upper respiratory illness
16 to ring out
17 personal pronoun referring to a male

HOMONYMS 161-170, PUZZLE 2

Use the clues to find the answers in the word search puzzle. Words can be found horizontally, vertically, or diagonally.

```
L  X  L  W  N  S  C  Y  C  M  Y  R  W  Z  V
E  W  S  E  L  G  I  P  Y  W  L  Z  Q  K  H
E  E  M  E  S  T  X  Z  O  N  F  H  Y  M  N
P  C  B  B  A  S  P  B  E  S  L  P  K  J  J
B  N  G  N  L  L  E  M  T  G  G  A  L  L  H
W  E  C  E  I  L  I  N  G  M  X  E  E  C  Y
W  D  M  F  F  N  E  N  D  C  F  U  X  P  B
K  I  T  M  D  D  D  N  G  N  C  L  F  L  N
J  S  U  W  I  W  G  W  E  L  F  F  K  E  N
K  E  A  S  D  X  K  W  T  Y  G  V  C  S  M
C  R  E  Q  O  P  R  B  V  Z  L  J  J  S  D
U  R  B  X  E  H  D  G  K  L  Q  V  T  O  C
V  L  N  W  S  M  M  D  E  N  I  M  Z  N  X
V  J  F  X  Y  I  M  R  P  N  M  E  P  L  W
J  S  I  G  H  S  M  J  N  L  Y  R  N  R  Z
```

_____ 1. to ring out
_____ 2. a tied ribbon
_____ 3. the upper surface of a room
_____ 4. a song of praise
_____ 5. 2 or more female deer
_____ 6. to dig in the earth, past tense
_____ 7. to sleep lightly
_____ 8. a house
_____ 9. to propel through the air, past tense
_____ 10. personal pronoun referring to a male
_____ 11. breaths that are long and loud
_____ 12. to decrease
_____ 13. French for a boyfriend
_____ 14. a concept that is taught
_____ 15. to seal or close something
_____ 16. to remove the exterior of something
_____ 17. tube or pipe used to convey heat or smoke outside
_____ 18. people who live in a home or community
_____ 19. how much something measures
_____ 20. short form of "influenza," an upper respiratory illness
_____ 21. the body part where our thoughts and memory reside

HOMONYMS 161-170, PUZZLE 3

Use the clues to find the answers in the crossword puzzle.

ACROSS

1 a song of praise
6 people who live in a home or community
8 a concept that is taught
10 to dig in the earth, past tense
12 to propel through the air, past tense
13 the upper surface of a room
15 French for a boyfriend
19 a house
20 short form of "influenza," an upper respiratory illness

DOWN

2 the body part where our thoughts and memory reside
3 to sleep lightly
4 to seal or close something
5 personal pronoun referring to a male
7 a tied ribbon
9 how much something measures
11 2 or more female deer
12 tube or pipe used to convey heat or smoke outside
14 to decrease
16 to ring out
17 breaths that are long and loud
18 to remove the exterior of something

107

HOMONYMS 161-170, PUZZLE 4

Use the clues to find the answers in the word search puzzle. Words can be found horizontally, vertically, or diagonally.

```
R  L  B  C  E  I  L  I  N  G  P  B  W
E  S  I  G  H  S  E  G  Q  R  S  O  M
S  F  L  T  V  G  E  L  G  T  B  I  N
I  E  M  A  Z  N  P  L  N  Z  N  F  R
D  P  A  W  E  L  F  E  E  D  L  U  P
E  J  V  L  W  P  D  S  U  V  B  A  T
N  Y  L  L  I  I  N  S  L  S  W  E  K
C  K  N  E  S  N  D  O  F  U  I  B  D
E  W  M  E  S  O  G  N  M  R  L  Z  O
Q  I  R  L  Z  S  F  H  Y  M  N  F  E
H  G  H  E  L  Z  E  N  G  R  P  W  S
R  L  K  H  C  H  F  N  G  V  Z  T  H
K  Q  D  E  N  I  M  P  Z  B  R  L  H
```

_____ 1. to decrease
_____ 2. a house
_____ 3. to ring out
_____ 4. a tied ribbon
_____ 5. the upper surface of a room
_____ 6. to sleep lightly
_____ 7/ a song of praise
_____ 8. to remove the exterior of something
_____ 9. 2 or more female deer
_____ 10. to dig in the earth, past tense
_____ 11. to propel through the air, past tense
_____ 12. breaths that are long and loud
_____ 13. French for a boyfriend
_____ 14. how much something measures
_____ 15. a concept that is taught
_____ 16. to seal or close something
_____ 17. personal pronoun referring to a male
_____ 18. tube or pipe used to convey heat or smoke outside
_____ 19. people who live in a home or community
_____ 20. short form of "influenza," an upper respiratory illness
_____ 21. the body part where our thoughts and memory reside

108

LESSON 18: HOMONYMS 171 - 180

171.	To: Too: Two:	A preposition. Adverb meaning extra or also. More than one, less than three.
172.	We: Wee: Whee:	A pronoun that includes a group plus oneself. An old term for small. An interjection that expresses excitement.
173.	Aught: Ought:	Zero. Should.
174.	Been: Ben: Bin:	To exist. A man's name, short for Benjamin. A box used for storing things.
175.	Cell: Sell:	A small simple room. A small part of a living organism. To exchange money for goods.
176.	Done: Dun:	To complete, past tense. A brownish gray color.
177.	Flour: Flower:	Finely ground grain used for baking. The colorful part of a plant.
178.	Hole: Whole:	A place in which something has been removed. Complete.
179.	Let's: Lets:	Contraction of *let* and *us*. Allows.
180.	Miner: Minor:	One who mines or digs in the earth. Someone who is underage.

Assignment Schedule for One-Year Course

Monday:	Give students the list above. Have them copy Groups 171-173 into their spelling notebook.
Tuesday:	Have students copy Groups 174-176 into their spelling notebook. Do Puzzle 1.
Wednesday:	Have students copy Groups 177-178 into their spelling notebook. Do Puzzle 2.
Thursday:	Have students copy Groups 179-180 into their spelling notebook. Do Puzzle 3.
Friday:	Do Puzzle 4 – without the lesson sheet or spelling notebook.
Friday fun:	Using some of these homonyms, write two rhyming couplets.

Assignment Schedule for Two-Year Course

Monday:	Give students the list above. Have them copy Groups 171-172 into their spelling notebook.
Tuesday:	Have students copy Groups 173-174 into their spelling notebook.
Wednesday:	Have students copy Groups 175-176 into their spelling notebook.
Thursday:	Have students copy Groups 177-178 into their spelling notebook.
Friday:	Have students copy Groups 179-180 into their spelling notebook.
Monday:	Do Puzzle 1.
Tuesday:	Do Puzzle 2.
Wednesday:	Do Puzzle 3.
Thursday:	Do Puzzle 4. – without the lesson sheet or spelling notebook.
Friday fun:	Using some of these homonyms, write two rhyming couplets.

Made with Crossword Weaver

HOMONYMS 171-180, PUZZLE 1

Use the clues to find the answers in the crossword puzzle.

ACROSS

3 a man's name, short for Benjamin
5 the colorful part of a plant
8 to complete, past tense
9 a pronoun that includes a group plus oneself
10 someone who is underage
14 a preposition
15 a brownish gray color
16 a box used for storing things
17 contraction of let and us
20 complete
21 allows

DOWN

1 a small part of a living organism
2 an interjection that expresses excitement
4 more than one, less than three
5 finely ground grain used for baking
6 an old term for small
7 to exist
10 one who mines or digs in the earth
11 should
12 a place in which something has been removed
13 zero
18 adverb meaning extra or also
19 to exchange money for goods

HOMONYMS 171-180, PUZZLE 2

Use the clues to find the answers in the word search puzzle. Words can be found horizontally, vertically, or diagonally.

```
N  U  D  R  B  C  M  I  N  O  R
R  W  H  O  L  E  E  B  I  N  L
E  T  T  H  G  U  A  L  B  K  E
W  T  W  O  R  B  M  M  L  N  T
O  D  S  O  E  W  T  Y  P  E  '
L  J  E  T  N  E  H  H  T  E  S
F  V  L  X  I  E  R  L  G  B  T
P  P  L  D  M  K  W  U  E  U  Z
R  N  O  W  N  H  O  L  O  T  O
C  N  F  E  E  O  O  W  K  L  S
E  B  B  E  T  H  T  N  E  H  F
```

_____ 1. zero
_____ 2. a preposition
_____ 3. an old term for small
_____ 4. allows
_____ 5. more than one, less than three
_____ 6. to exist
_____ 7. the colorful part of a plant
_____ 8. an interjection that expresses excitement
_____ 9. should
_____ 10. a man's name, short for Benjamin
_____ 11. adverb meaning extra or also
_____ 12. to exchange money for goods
_____ 13. one who mines or digs in the earth
_____ 14. a box used for storing things
_____ 15. to complete, past tense
_____ 16. a brownish gray color
_____ 17. finely ground grain used for baking
_____ 18. complete
_____ 19. contraction of *let* and *us*
_____ 20. someone who is underage
_____ 21. a small part of a living organism
_____ 22. a place in which something has been removed
_____ 23. a pronoun that includes a group plus oneself

112

HOMONYMS 171-180, PUZZLE 3

Use the clues to find the answers in the crossword puzzle.

ACROSS

2 more than one, less than three
4 a small part of a living organism
5 allows
8 an interjection that expresses excitement
9 complete
10 a preposition
12 finely ground grain used for baking
13 to complete, past tense
14 a man's name, short for Benjamin
15 adverb meaning extra or also
17 a pronoun that includes a group plus oneself
18 one who mines or digs in the earth
19 a box used for storing things

DOWN

1 the colorful part of a plant
3 an old term for small
5 contraction of let and us
6 to exchange money for goods
7 a place in which something has been removed
11 zero
13 a brownish gray color
14 to exist
16 should
18 someone who is underage

HOMONYMS 171-180, PUZZLE 4

Use the clues to find the answers in the word search puzzle. Words can be found
horizontally, vertically, or diagonally.

```
C  N  U  D  K  T  H  G  U  A  W  R
N  N  B  W  T  W  O  F  G  H  J  O
D  B  I  N  E  W  T  L  E  Z  T  N
F  R  N  L  N  Q  V  E  Y  Y  J  I
O  H  M  D  E  L  W  H  O  L  E  M
T  T  O  L  E  T  O  X  R  N  R  W
R  N  O  X  B  O  S  P  E  Z  E  E
E  H  R  T  T  K  C  B  G  S  W  E
N  Z  W  U  H  T  Z  E  H  E  O  N
I  F  M  K  O  G  Z  K  L  L  L  Q
M  X  C  N  K  L  U  Z  K  L  F  T
T  S  '  T  E  L  F  O  W  L  Z  N
```

_____ 1. zero

_____ 2. should

_____ 3. a preposition

_____ 4. a brownish gray color

_____ 5. to exist

_____ 6. an old term for small

_____ 7. allows

_____ 8. more than one, less than three

_____ 9. the colorful part of a plant

_____ 10. a man's name, short for Benjamin

_____ 11. complete

_____ 12. adverb meaning extra or also

_____ 13. a small part of a living organism

_____ 14. to exchange money for goods

_____ 15. one who mines or digs in the earth

_____ 16. a box used for storing things

_____ 17. to complete, past tense

_____ 18. finely ground grain used for baking

_____ 19. contraction of *let* and *us*

_____ 20. an interjection that expresses excitement

_____ 21. someone who is underage

_____ 22. a place in which something has been removed

_____ 23. a pronoun that includes a group plus oneself

114   Made with 1-2-3 Word Search Maker

LESSON 19: HOMONYMS 181 - 190

181.	Pedal: Peddle: Petal:	A foot handle that is used to move a bike forward. To sell. To advertise or publicize. Part of a flower that radiates from the center.
182.	Review: Revue:	To look over. A theatrical production made up of short skits.
183.	Slew: Slough:	To slay (or kill),past tense. Deep muddy area; swamp.
184.	Toe: Tow:	One of the digits on a human foot. To pull behind.
185.	Weak: Week:	Not strong. 7 days.
186.	Away: Aweigh:	To leave an area. To raise an anchor off the bottom of the sea (or bay).
187.	Beer: Bier:	An alcoholic beverage. A flat surface on which a body is placed.
188.	Censor: Sensor:	A person who monitors public morals and publications. Something that registers an activity.
189.	Dual: Duel:	Two things working together. A fight, typically between two men with pistols or swords (match the "e" with "each other").
190.	For Fore: Four:	A preposition meaning in favor of or on behalf of. The front. The number between 3 and 5.

Assignment Schedule for One-Year Course

Monday:	Give students the list above. Have them copy Groups 181-183 into their spelling notebook.
Tuesday:	Have students copy Groups 184-186 into their spelling notebook. Do Puzzle 1.
Wednesday:	Have students copy Groups 187-188 into their spelling notebook. Do Puzzle 2.
Thursday:	Have students copy Groups 189-190 into their spelling notebook. Do Puzzle 3.
Friday:	Do Puzzle 4 – without the lesson sheet or spelling notebook.
Friday fun:	Using the homonyms above, write a short story about a bicycle. You can make this nonfiction or fiction (fantasy). Have fun with it

Assignment Schedule for Two-Year Course

Monday:	Give students the list above. Have them copy Groups 181-182 into their spelling notebook.
Tuesday:	Have students copy Groups 183-184 into their spelling notebook.
Wednesday:	Have students copy Groups 185-186 into their spelling notebook.
Thursday:	Have students copy Groups 187-188 into their spelling notebook.
Friday:	Have students copy Groups 189-190 into their spelling notebook.
Monday:	Do Puzzle 1.
Tuesday:	Do Puzzle 2.
Wednesday:	Do Puzzle 3.
Thursday:	Do Puzzle 4. – without the lesson sheet or spelling notebook.
Friday fun:	Using the homonyms above, write a short story about a bicycle. You can make this nonfiction or fiction (fantasy). Have fun with it

HOMONYMS 181-190, PUZZLE 1

Use the clues to find the answers in the crossword puzzle.

ACROSS

3 to leave an area
5 an alcoholic beverage
6 deep muddy area; swamp
8 7 days
9 a theatrical production made up of short skits
10 to slay (or kill),past tense
11 part of a flower that radiates from the center
12 the number between 3 and 5
13 one of the digits on a human foot
14 to look over
15 two things working together
16 a person who monitors public morals and publications

DOWN

1 to raise an anchor off the bottom of the sea (or bay)
2 a fight, typically between two men with pistols or swords
4 the front
5 a flat surface on which a body is placed
6 something that registers an activity
7 a foot handle that is used to move a bike forward
8 not strong
11 to sell; to advertise or publicize
12 a preposition meaning in favor of or on behalf of
13 to pull behind

117

HOMONYMS 181-190, PUZZLE 2

Use the clues to find the answers in the word search puzzle. Words can be found horizontally, vertically, or diagonally.

```
R  W  T  W  X  N  H  G  U  O  L  S
R  E  I  B  F  O  R  E  T  K  R  E
X  R  G  S  P  E  T  A  L  O  L  K
X  R  L  W  E  E  K  N  F  D  B  R
K  E  E  A  Q  L  Z  P  D  E  K  H
W  V  U  W  M  A  N  E  E  X  W  K
M  U  D  E  R  D  P  R  A  S  Y  K
E  E  W  I  J  E  T  L  E  W  A  G
F  O  O  G  P  P  V  N  A  E  A  G
Q  O  T  H  B  D  S  I  W  U  N  Y
L  C  U  B  R  O  S  N  E  C  D  L
X  L  K  R  R  N  F  M  T  W  T  H
```

_____ 1. to sell; to advertise or publicize
_____ 2. 7 days
_____ 3. a flat surface on which a body is placed
_____ 4. the number between 3 and 5
_____ 5. to look over
_____ 6. to slay (or kill),past tense
_____ 7. two things working together
_____ 8. to pull behind
_____ 9. not strong
_____ 10. something that registers an activity
_____ 11. the front
_____ 12. deep muddy area; swamp
_____ 13. to leave an area
_____ 14. a foot handle that is used to move a bike forward
_____ 15. an alcoholic beverage
_____ 16. one of the digits on a human foot
_____ 17. a person who monitors public morals and publications
_____ 18. a theatrical production made up of short skits
_____ 19. part of a flower that radiates from the center
_____ 20. a fight, typically between two men with pistols or swords
_____ 21. a preposition meaning in favor of or on behalf of
_____ 22. to raise an anchor off the bottom of the sea (or bay)

HOMONYMS 181-190, PUZZLE 3

Use the clues to find the answers in the crossword puzzle.

ACROSS

3 one of the digits on a human foot
4 a theatrical production made up of short skits
5 to leave an area
7 the front
9 a foot handle that is used to move a bike forward
11 something that registers an activity
14 to sell; to advertise or publicize
15 to pull behind
16 deep muddy area; swamp
17 an alcoholic beverage
18 a fight, typically between two men with pistols or swords

DOWN

1 the number between 3 and 5
2 part of a flower that radiates from the center
4 to look over
6 7 days
7 a preposition meaning in favor of or on behalf of
8 not strong
10 to raise an anchor off the bottom of the sea (or bay)
12 to slay (or kill), past tense
13 a person who monitors public morals and publications
17 a flat surface on which a body is placed
18 two things working together

 Made with Crossword Weaver

HOMONYMS 181-190, PUZZLE 4

Use the clues to find the answers in the word search puzzle. Words can be found horizontally, vertically, or diagonally.

```
R   T   J   L   F   E   H   G   U   O   L   S
E   M   T   A   L   E   C   E   N   S   O   R
V   M   D   D   W   K   O   B   L   G   F   A
U   F   D   E   O   M   E   T   K   R   O   W
E   E   O   P   T   E   R   A   M   K   U   E
P   H   R   R   R   E   O   W   C   R   I
C   K   N   W   E   W   E   B   S   A   M   G
W   N   W   E   E   K   N   V   V   N   Y   H
L   W   R   E   I   B   M   S   I   Q   E   N
A   P   E   T   A   L   L   R   M   E   L   S
U   T   C   L   Q   E   O   W   D   N   W   L
D   Q   G   T   W   F   M   D   U   E   L   R
```

_____ 1. 7 days
_____ 2. two things working together
_____ 3. to raise an anchor off the bottom of the sea (or bay)
_____ 4. a flat surface on which a body is placed
_____ 5. the number between 3 and 5
_____ 6. to slay (or kill),past tense
_____ 7. to pull behind
_____ 8. not strong
_____ 9. something that registers an activity
_____ 10. a person who monitors public morals and publications
_____ 11. the front
_____ 12. deep muddy area; swamp
_____ 13. to sell; to advertise or publicize
_____ 14. to leave an area
_____ 15. a foot handle that is used to move a bike forward
_____ 16. one of the digits on a human foot
_____ 17. a theatrical production made up of short skits
_____ 18. part of a flower that radiates from the center
_____ 19. an alcoholic beverage
_____ 20. to look over
_____ 21, a fight, typically between two men with pistols or swords
_____ 22. a preposition meaning in favor of or on behalf of

120

LESSON 20: HOMONYMS 191 - 200

191.	Hour: Our:	60 minutes. Possessive pronoun showing ownership by a group including oneself.
192.	Liar: Lyre:	One who tells falsehoods. A stringed instrument from ancient Greece.
193.	Might: Mite:	An auxiliary (or helping) verb. A tiny, eight-legged insect that carries diseases.
194.	Peer: Pier:	To look at. (The two "Es" are for "eyes.") A walkway that extends from the shore into a body of water.
195.	Rigger: Rigor: Rigueur:	One who rigs (or prepares things for use). High degree of difficulty, high expectations. Fever or chills. Part of the term "de rigueur" and means required by custom or fashion.
196.	Sloe: Slow:	Small, round, dark fruit of the blackthorn. To move at an unhurried pace.
197.	Trader: Traitor:	One who trades. One who has betrayed others.
198.	Weather: Whether:	Conditions in the atmosphere. If.
199.	Aye: Eye: I:	Formal way of saying or voting "yes." Bodily organ used for sight. First person personal pronoun; refers to oneself.
200.	Berry: Bury:	A small fruit that grows on low bushes. To put in the ground; to hide.

Assignment Schedule for One-Year Course

Monday:	Give students the list above. Have them copy Groups 191-193 into their spelling notebook.
Tuesday:	Have students copy Groups 194-196 into their spelling notebook. Do Puzzle 1.
Wednesday:	Have students copy Groups 197-198 into their spelling notebook. Do Puzzle 2.
Thursday:	Have students copy Groups 199-200 into their spelling notebook. Do Puzzle 3.
Friday:	Do Puzzle 4 – without the lesson sheet or spelling notebook.
Friday fun:	How would you feel about writing a story about a trader who travels by schooner (on the ocean) or prairie schooner (wagon on the prairie). Have some fun with this

Assignment Schedule for Two-Year Course

Monday:	Give students the list above. Have them copy Groups 191-192 into their spelling notebook.
Tuesday:	Have students copy Groups 193-194 into their spelling notebook.
Wednesday:	Have students copy Groups 195-196 into their spelling notebook.
Thursday:	Have students copy Groups 197-198 into their spelling notebook.
Friday:	Have students copy Groups 199-200 into their spelling notebook.
Monday:	Do Puzzle 1.
Tuesday:	Do Puzzle 2.
Wednesday:	Do Puzzle 3.
Thursday:	Do Puzzle 4. – without the lesson sheet or spelling notebook.
Friday fun:	How would you feel about writing a story about a trader who travels by schooner (on the ocean) or prairie schooner (wagon on the prairie). Have some fun with this

HOMONYMS 191-200, PUZZLE 1

Use the clues to find the answers in the crossword puzzle.

ACROSS

5 an auxiliary (or helping) verb
7 formal way of saying or voting "yes"
8 high degree of difficulty, high expectations
9 part of the term "de rigueur;" something required by custom
11 bodily organ used for sight
13 if
14 one who has betrayed others
17 one who rigs (or prepares things for use)
19 a stringed instrument from ancient Greece
20 to put in the ground; to hide

DOWN

1 a walkway that extends from the shore into a body of water
2 one who tells falsehoods
3 small, round, dark fruit of the blackthorn
4 60 minutes
6 one who trades
10 to look at
12 a tiny, eight-legged insect that carries diseases
13 conditions in the atmosphere
15 possessive pronoun showing ownership by a group including oneself
16 a small fruit that grows on low bushes
18 to move at an unhurried pace

Made with Crossword Weaver

HOMONYMS 191-200, PUZZLE 2

Use the clues to find the answers in the word search puzzle. Words can be found horizontally, vertically, or diagonally.

```
N  L  N  N  B  E  R  R  Y  M  T  D
T  I  Y  K  T  W  L  L  I  R  K  V
R  E  F  R  N  W  R  T  A  I  R  W
S  E  Y  M  E  U  E  D  L  G  E  E
B  L  I  A  O  H  E  K  L  U  G  A
Z  W  O  P  D  R  M  B  Y  E  G  T
T  H  C  W  Y  R  I  C  L  U  I  H
X  E  G  M  R  U  G  Z  M  R  R  E
R  T  D  M  U  O  H  S  L  O  E  R
K  H  C  Q  B  H  T  C  G  H  M  E
Y  E  R  E  E  P  L  I  A  R  K  Y
R  R  O  T  I  A  R  T  Q  Q  V  E
```

_____ 1. 60 minutes
_____ 2. if
_____ 3. to look at
_____ 4. to move at an unhurried pace
_____ 5. one who tells falsehoods
_____ 6. one who rigs (or prepares things for use)
_____ 7. an auxiliary (or helping) verb
_____ 8. to put in the ground; to hide
_____ 9. bodily organ used for sight
_____ 10. a tiny, eight-legged insect that carries diseases
_____ 11. a walkway that extends from the shore into a body of water
_____ 12. high degree of difficulty, high expectations
_____ 13. small, round, dark fruit of the blackthorn
_____ 14. one who trades
_____ 15. a stringed instrument from ancient Greece
_____ 16. conditions in the atmosphere
_____ 17. formal way of saying or voting "yes"
_____ 18. first person personal pronoun; refers to oneself
_____ 19. a small fruit that grows on low bushes
_____ 20. one who has betrayed others
_____ 21. part of the term "de rigueur;" something required by custom
_____ 22. possessive pronoun showing ownership by a group including oneself

HOMONYMS 191-200, PUZZLE 3

Use the clues to find the answers in the crossword puzzle.

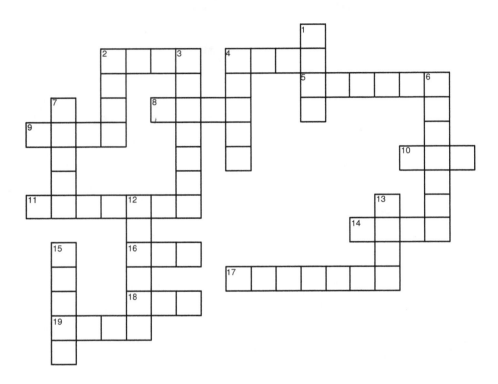

ACROSS

2 to move at an unhurried pace
4 to put in the ground; to hide
5 one who rigs (or prepares things for use)
8 to look at
9 a tiny, eight-legged insect that carries diseases
10 possessive pronoun showing ownership by a group including oneself
11 one who has betrayed others
14 one who tells falsehoods
16 formal way of saying or voting "yes"
17 conditions in the atmosphere
18 bodily organ used for sight
19 60 minutes

DOWN

1 a stringed instrument from ancient Greece
2 small, round, dark fruit of the blackthorn
3 if
4 a small fruit that grows on low bushes
6 part of the term "de rigueur;" something required by custom
7 high degree of difficulty, high expectations
12 one who trades
13 a walkway that extends from the shore into a body of water
15 an auxiliary (or helping) verb

125   Made with Crossword Weaver

HOMONYMS 191-200, PUZZLE 4

Use the clues to find the answers in the word search puzzle. Words can be found horizontally, vertically, or diagonally.

```
Y  R  E  D  A  R  T  E  K  C  B
S  R  O  T  I  A  R  T  Y  M  I
K  L  R  X  M  Q  C  L  R  E  R
T  W  O  E  R  E  E  P  Y  O  W
W  M  E  E  B  A  M  R  G  R  H
R  I  R  A  Y  I  U  I  U  R  E
U  G  C  E  T  B  R  O  L  E  T
O  H  Y  E  I  H  W  F  S  G  H
H  T  F  V  T  P  E  C  L  G  E
V  R  I  G  U  E  U  R  O  I  R
X  Z  X  R  L  I  A  R  W  R  M
```

_____ 1. if

_____ 2. to look at

_____ 3. 60 minutes

_____ 4. an auxiliary (or helping) verb

_____ 5. to move at an unhurried pace

_____ 6. one who trades

_____ 7. one who tells falsehoods

_____ 8. to put in the ground; to hide

_____ 9. bodily organ used for sight

_____ 10. a tiny, eight-legged insect that carries diseases

_____ 11. conditions in the atmosphere

_____ 12. part of the term "de rigueur;" something required by custom

_____ 13. a walkway that extends from the shore into a body of water

_____ 14. high degree of difficulty, high expectations

_____ 15. small, round, dark fruit of the blackthorn

_____ 16. one who rigs (or prepares things for use)

_____ 17. one who has betrayed others

_____ 18. a stringed instrument from ancient Greece

_____ 19. formal way of saying or voting "yes"

_____ 20. first person personal pronoun; refers to oneself

_____ 21. a small fruit that grows on low bushes

_____ 22. possessive pronoun showing ownership by a group including oneself

LESSON 21: HOMONYMS 201 - 210

201.	Cent: Sent:	A penny. To send someone/something elsewhere, past tense.
202.	Foreword: Forward:	An introductory part of a book, written by someone other than the author. Move ahead.
203.	Humorous: Humerus:	Something that is funny. The bone in the upper arm.
204.	Lie: Lye:	An untruth or falsehood. A strong substance used in homemade soap.
205.	Missal: Missile:	A book that contains all of the church services for a year. Something that is hurled at (or launched toward) an object.
206.	Pi: Pie:	A geometric measurement, roughly 22/7. A sweet dessert baked on a crust in a circular pan.
207.	Right: Rite: -Wright: Write:	Correct; opposite of left. A ritual. A craftsman, such as a playwright or wheelwright. To put pen to paper.
208.	Soar: Sore:	To fly high. A painful place. To be in pain.
209.	Which: Witch:	Choose between two possibilities. Member of the Wiccan faith.
210.	Berth: Birth:	A room on a ship or train. To bring to life.

Assignment Schedule for One-Year Course

Monday:	Give students the list above. Have them copy Groups 201-203 into their spelling notebook.
Tuesday:	Have students copy Groups 204-206 into their spelling notebook. Do Puzzle 1.
Wednesday:	Have students copy Groups 207-208 into their spelling notebook. Do Puzzle 2.
Thursday:	Have students copy Groups 209-210 into their spelling notebook. Do Puzzle 3.
Friday:	Do Puzzle 4 – without the lesson sheet or spelling notebook.
Friday fun:	Using some of these homonyms, write something humorous. This can be a paragraph or a poem. Your choice.

Assignment Schedule for Two-Year Course

Monday:	Give students the list above. Have them copy Groups 201-202 into their spelling notebook.
Tuesday:	Have students copy Groups 203-204 into their spelling notebook.
Wednesday:	Have students copy Groups 205-206 into their spelling notebook.
Thursday:	Have students copy Groups 207-208 into their spelling notebook.
Friday:	Have students copy Groups 209-210 into their spelling notebook.
Monday:	Do Puzzle 1.
Tuesday:	Do Puzzle 2.
Wednesday:	Do Puzzle 3.
Thursday:	Do Puzzle 4. – without the lesson sheet or spelling notebook.
Friday fun:	Using some of these homonyms, write something humorous. This can be a paragraph or a poem. Your choice.

Homonyms 201-210, Puzzle 1

Use the clues to find the answers in the crossword puzzle.

ACROSS

2 a book that contains all of the church services for a year
5 choose between two possibilities
7 move ahead
9 a penny
10 to bring to life
13 an untruth or falsehood
14 to put pen to paper
16 something that is hurled at an object
18 correct; opposite of left
19 a craftsman, such as a playwright or wheelwright
20 to send someone/something elsewhere, past tense

DOWN

1 member of the wiccan faith
3 to fly high
4 an introduction in a book, written by someone other than the author
6 something that is funny
8 a painful place. to be in pain
10 a room on a ship or train
11 a ritual
12 the bone in the upper arm
13 a strong substance used in homemade soap
15 a geometric measurement, roughly 22/7
17 a sweet dessert baked on a crust in a circular pan

129 Made with Crossword Weaver

HOMONYMS 201-210, PUZZLE 2

Use the clues to find the answers in the word search puzzle. Words can be found horizontally, vertically, or diagonally.

```
J  J  B  F  I  B  P  I  E  V  K  T
H  W  C  P  E  I  L  M  L  T  W  H
F  C  I  F  O  R  E  W  O  R  D  U
R  O  I  T  T  J  T  I  Q  L  M
T  I  R  H  C  H  P  G  I  H  Y  O
N  M  G  W  W  H  H  H  U  R  R  R
E  E  T  H  A  T  T  M  J  L  W  O
C  R  Y  R  T  R  E  P  J  A  R  U
V  I  P  L  E  R  D  E  T  S  A  S
L  T  V  B  U  Y  R  N  M  S  O  Q
T  E  K  S  T  O  E  J  M  I  S  M
L  E  L  I  S  S  I  M  Q  M  X  X
```

_____ 1. to fly high
_____ 2. a penny
_____ 3. move ahead
_____ 4. something that is funny
_____ 5. a geometric measurement, roughly 22/7
_____ 6. correct; opposite of left
_____ 7. to bring to life
_____ 8. the bone in the upper arm
_____ 9. a ritual
_____ 10. an untruth or falsehood
_____ 11. choose between two possibilities
_____ 12. something that is hurled at an object
_____ 13. a sweet dessert baked on a crust in a circular pan
_____ 14. to put pen to paper
_____ 15. a painful place. to be in pain
_____ 16. member of the Wiccan faith
_____ 17. a strong substance used in homemade soap
_____ 18. a room on a ship or train
_____ 19. to send someone/something elsewhere, past tense
_____ 20. a book that contains all of the church services for a year
_____ 21. a craftsman, such as a playwright or wheelwright
_____ 22. an introduction in a book, written by someone other than the author

HOMONYMS 201-210, PUZZLE 3

Use the clues to find the answers in the crossword puzzle.

ACROSS

2 a book that contains all of the church services for a year
4 a craftsman, such as a playwright or wheelwright
5 an introduction in a book, written by someone other than the author
7 choose between two possibilities
9 a ritual
12 a strong substance used in homemade soap
13 the bone in the upper arm
14 a painful place. to be in pain
15 to bring to life
16 to send someone/something elsewhere, past tense
17 a geometric measurement, roughly 22/7
18 a penny

DOWN

1 a sweet dessert baked on a crust in a circular pan
3 to fly high
4 to put pen to paper
5 move ahead
6 member of the wiccan faith
8 something that is funny
9 correct; opposite of left
10 something that is hurled at an object
11 a room on a ship or train
12 an untruth or falsehood

HOMONYMS 201-210, PUZZLE 4

Use the clues to find the answers in the word search puzzle. Words can be found horizontally, vertically, or diagonally.

```
K  P  P  R  E  K  M  B  H  Q  T  K  R
J  M  I  R  P  H  I  U  F  C  N  X  W
J  T  O  E  Q  R  M  T  K  F  E  M  T
E  S  R  L  T  E  N  L  V  X  C  W  L
T  R  Z  H  R  E  Y  R  B  H  H  H  A
F  A  K  U  S  T  H  G  I  R  W  U  S
L  O  S  F  O  R  E  W  O  R  D  M  S
B  S  R  W  X  L  H  T  R  J  W  O  I
E  Y  F  W  I  E  B  N  I  K  N  R  M
R  X  L  S  A  T  Y  N  G  R  B  O  M
T  N  S  B  R  R  C  L  H  T  W  U  X
H  I  E  I  L  R  D  H  T  J  M  S  Q
M  W  H  I  C  H  Q  Q  Z  P  I  J  T
```

_____ 1. a ritual
_____ 2. to fly high
_____ 3. a penny
_____ 4. move ahead
_____ 5. correct; opposite of left
_____ 6. to bring to life
_____ 7. a room on a ship or train
_____ 8. the bone in the upper arm
_____ 9. an untruth or falsehood
_____ 10. something that is funny
_____ 11. choose between two possibilities
_____ 12. a craftsman, such as a playwright or wheelwright
_____ 13. something that is hurled at an object
_____ 14. to put pen to paper
_____ 15. a painful place. to be in pain
_____ 16. member of the Wiccan faith
_____ 17. a sweet dessert baked on a crust in a circular pan
_____ 18. a strong substance used in homemade soap
_____ 19. a geometric measurement, roughly 22/7
_____ 20. to send someone/something elsewhere, past tense
_____ 21. a book that contains all of the church services for a year
_____ 22. an introduction in a book, written by someone other than the author

LESSON 22: HOMONYMS 211 - 220

211.	Cents: Scents: Sense: Since:	More than one penny. Smells. Intelligence or one of the five ways living things understand their environment. Because.
212.	Forth: Fourth:	Onward, forward. Out in the open, into the world. Ordinal number between third and fifth.
213.	Links: Lynx:	Connections to other things. Another name for a bobcat.
214.	Moat: Mote:	A body of water that surrounds a castle. An old word for a speck.
215.	Picture: Pitcher:	An image taken with a camera. A large vessel into which several cups of beverage are placed & stored.
216.	Ring: Wring:	A band or circle. A piece of jewelry worn on a finger. To twist something.
217.	Sole: Soul:	Only. A type of fish. Bottom of the foot. The internal part of a person, not related to the body.
218.	While: Wile:	During. Cunning intelligence. To lazily pass time.
219.	Better: Bettor:	A positive description of quality. One who places bets.
220.	Chile: Chili: Chilly:	A country in South America. A spicy stew made of tomatoes, ground beef, and red beans. Cool or cold.

Assignment Schedule for One-Year Course

Monday:	Give students the list above. Have them copy Groups 211-213 into their spelling notebook.
Tuesday:	Have students copy Groups 214-216 into their spelling notebook. Do Puzzle 1.
Wednesday:	Have students copy Groups 217-218 into their spelling notebook. Do Puzzle 2.
Thursday:	Have students copy Groups 219-220 into their spelling notebook. Do Puzzle 3.
Friday:	Do Puzzle 4 – without the lesson sheet or spelling notebook.
Friday fun:	Using some of these homonyms, write a fable about a lynx.

Assignment Schedule for Two-Year Course

Monday:	Give students the list above. Have them copy Groups 211-212 into their spelling notebook.
Tuesday:	Have students copy Groups 213-214 into their spelling notebook.
Wednesday:	Have students copy Groups 215-216 into their spelling notebook.
Thursday:	Have students copy Groups 217-218 into their spelling notebook.
Friday:	Have students copy Groups 219-220 into their spelling notebook.
Monday:	Do Puzzle 1.
Tuesday:	Do Puzzle 2.
Wednesday:	Do Puzzle 3.
Thursday:	Do Puzzle 4. – without the lesson sheet or spelling notebook.
Friday fun:	Using some of these homonyms, write a fable about a lynx.

HOMONYMS 211-220, PUZZLE 1

Use the clues to find the answers in the crossword puzzle.

ACROSS

2 ordinal number between third and fifth
3 cunning intelligence
6 an old word for a speck
7 connections to other things
10 one who places bets
11 an image taken with a camera
14 more than one penny
16 a spicy stew made of tomatoes, ground beef, and red beans
17 a band or circle. a piece of jewelry worn on a finger
18 another name for a bobcat
19 one of the five ways living things understand their environment.

DOWN

1 the internal part of a person, not related to the body
3 during
4 only. a type of fish. bottom of the foot
5 a body of water that surrounds a castle
8 because
9 onward, forward. out in the open, into the world
10 a positive description of quality
11 a large vessel that holds several cups of beverage
12 a country in south America
13 to twist something
14 cool or cold
15 smells

135

HOMONYMS 211-220, PUZZLE 2

Use the clues to find the answers in the word search puzzle. Words can be found horizontally, vertically, or diagonally.

```
Q  R  C  T  J  Y  L  X  S  E  N  S  E
E  I  H  A  R  G  C  E  L  X  D  F  S
L  N  I  O  M  G  L  Q  W  U  O  L  T
I  G  L  M  R  I  P  R  F  U  O  G  N
H  L  L  X  W  C  I  I  R  W  T  S  E
W  P  Y  R  N  N  H  T  T  Y  G  W  C
C  C  T  R  G  Y  H  I  S  C  E  G  P
H  S  K  N  I  L  L  T  L  T  H  T  F
I  S  K  J  X  X  N  J  O  E  M  E  O
L  L  I  H  Q  E  Q  M  E  L  O  S  R
I  F  L  N  C  P  I  C  T  U  R  E  T
L  D  M  S  C  T  B  E  T  T  O  R  H
F  Y  X  P  B  E  B  E  T  T  E  R  K
```

_____ 1. smells
_____ 2. another name for a bobcat
_____ 3. cool or cold
_____ 4. during
_____ 5. because
_____ 6. ordinal number between third and fifth
_____ 7. connections to other things
_____ 8. only. a type of fish. bottom of the foot
_____ 9. an old word for a speck
_____ 10. an image taken with a camera
_____ 11. more than one penny
_____ 12. onward, forward. out in the open, into the world
_____ 13. a band or circle. a piece of jewelry worn on a finger
_____ 14. a country in south America
_____ 15. to twist something
_____ 16. the internal part of a person, not related to the body
_____ 17. cunning intelligence
_____ 18. a positive description of quality
_____ 19. a body of water that surrounds a castle
_____ 20. one who places bets
_____ 21. one of the five ways living things understand their environment.
_____ 22. a large vessel that holds several cups of beverage
_____ 23. a spicy stew made of tomatoes, ground beef, and red beans

136

HOMONYMS 211-220, PUZZLE 3

Use the clues to find the answers in the crossword puzzle.

ACROSS

2 only. a type of fish. bottom of the foot
5 cool or cold
6 an image taken with a camera
8 another name for a bobcat
9 because
12 a country in south America
15 one who places bets
16 the internal part of a person, not related to the body
18 to twist something
19 a large vessel that holds several cups of beverage
20 a band or circle. a piece of jewelry worn on a finger
21 onward, forward. out in the open, into the world
22 smells

DOWN

1 a body of water that surrounds a castle
3 during
4 one of the five ways living things understand their environment.
7 a spicy stew made of tomatoes, ground beef, and red beans
10 more than one penny
11 a positive description of quality
13 ordinal number between third and fifth
14 an old word for a speck
17 connections to other things
18 cunning intelligence

HOMONYMS 211-220, PUZZLE 4

Use the clues to find the answers in the word search puzzle. Words can be found horizontally, vertically, or diagonally.

```
R  C  H  I  L  L  Y  N  S  K  N  I  L
O  R  C  W  G  D  T  T  E  L  O  S
T  S  H  P  Z  K  N  X  Z  Z  J  X  K
T  F  I  Y  I  E  S  E  N  S  E  R  Z
E  O  L  N  C  T  R  C  F  Y  Z  I  E
B  R  I  S  C  W  C  O  R  R  L  N  L
T  T  W  K  R  E  U  H  L  K  M  G  I
T  H  G  I  L  R  S  C  E  R  B  Z  H
A  R  N  I  T  Y  T  L  H  R  T  E  W
O  G  W  H  L  F  N  L  P  I  T  D  V
M  K  B  E  T  T  E  R  U  O  L  D  T
N  D  K  R  R  D  C  L  M  O  G  E  Q
P  I  C  T  U  R  E  N  V  B  S  V  P
```

_____ 1. smells
_____ 2. cool or cold
_____ 3. during
_____ 4. an image taken with a camera
_____ 5. to twist something
_____ 6. because
_____ 7. ordinal number between third and fifth
_____ 8. a large vessel that holds several cups of beverage
_____ 9. one who places bets
_____ 10. connections to other things
_____ 11. only. a type of fish. bottom of the foot
_____ 12. an old word for a speck
_____ 13. more than one penny
_____ 14. onward, forward. out in the open, into the world
_____ 15. a country in south America
_____ 16. the internal part of a person, not related to the body
_____ 17. cunning intelligence
_____ 18. a band or circle. a piece of jewelry worn on a finger
_____ 19. a positive description of quality
_____ 20. a body of water that surrounds a castle
_____ 21. another name for a bobcat
_____ 22. one of the five ways living things understand their environment.
_____ 23. a spicy stew made of tomatoes, ground beef, and red beans

LESSON 23: HOMONYMS 221 - 230

221.	Foul: Fowl:	Bad smelling. Outside the margins, like a foul ball. Poultry, such as chicken or turkey. (Match the "w" with wings.)
222.	Load: Lode:	To fill something. Weight/cargo. A mineral deposit.
223.	Mode: Mowed:	A method. To cut down something (like grass), past tense.
224.	Plain: Plane:	Something simple, without adornment. Clear/evident. An aircraft; a geometric concept of two dimensions.
225.	Road: Rode: Rowed:	A path. Form of ride, past tense. Move a boat through water using an oar, past tense.
226.	Some: Sum:	Part of something or a group. Total.
227.	Whine: Wine:	To moan in a high pitched voice. An alcoholic beverage typically made from grapes or berries.
228.	Billed: Build:	To be told what you owe, past tense. To construct.
229.	Chute: Shoot:	A slope to drop things down. To fire a weapon.
230.	Loan: Lone:	To lend something to another. A solitary being.

Assignment Schedule for One-Year Course

Monday:	Give students the list above. Have them copy Groups 221-223 into their spelling notebook..
Tuesday:	Have students copy Groups 224-226 into their spelling notebook. Do Puzzle 1.
Wednesday:	Have students copy Groups 227-228 into their spelling notebook. Do Puzzle 2.
Thursday:	Have students copy Groups 229-230 into their spelling notebook. Do Puzzle 3.
Friday:	Do Puzzle 4 – without the lesson sheet or spelling notebook.
Friday fun:	Using some of these homonyms, write a quatrain.

Assignment Schedule for Two-Year Course

Monday:	Give students the list above. Have them copy Groups 221-222 into their spelling notebook..
Tuesday:	Have students copy Groups 223-224 into their spelling notebook.
Wednesday:	Have students copy Groups 225-226 into their spelling notebook.
Thursday:	Have students copy Groups 227-228 into their spelling notebook.
Friday:	Have students copy Groups 229-230 into their spelling notebook.
Monday:	Do Puzzle 1.
Tuesday:	Do Puzzle 2.
Wednesday:	Do Puzzle 3.
Thursday:	Do Puzzle 4. – without the lesson sheet or spelling notebook.
Friday fun:	Using some of these homonyms, write a quatrain.

HOMONYMS 221-230, PUZZLE 1

Use the clues to find the answers in the crossword puzzle.

ACROSS

1 bad smelling; outside the margins
4 a method
5 poultry
8 to construct
10 part of something or a group
11 an aircraft; a geometric concept of two dimensions
13 to cut down something (like grass), past tense
15 to be told what you owe, past tense
17 form of ride, past tense
18 something simple, without adornment; clear/evident

DOWN

2 a mineral deposit
3 move a boat through water using an oar, past tense
6 an alcoholic beverage typically made from grapes or berries
7 a slope to drop things down
9 a solitary being
10 total
12 to fill something. weight/cargo
14 to moan in a high pitched voice
16 to lend something to another
17 a path

Made with Crossword Weaver

HOMONYMS 221-230, PUZZLE 2

Use the clues to find the answers in the word search puzzle. Words can be found horizontally, vertically, or diagonally.

```
D  L  I  U  B  K  N  I  A  L  P
C  G  R  O  W  E  D  W  M  D  F
H  X  L  E  L  N  H  D  O  E  T
U  Y  U  W  N  I  A  K  D  L  S
T  N  O  M  N  A  D  O  E  L  U
E  F  F  E  M  G  L  D  L  I  M
K  D  R  O  Z  E  O  P  V  B  D
N  S  W  W  N  R  L  K  K  Z  A
Y  E  O  O  D  S  H  O  O  T  O
D  N  L  M  P  L  M  X  D  G  R
L  O  A  D  E  N  I  W  Q  E  B
```

_____ 1. total
_____ 2. poultry
_____ 3. to fill something. weight/cargo
_____ 4. to construct
_____ 5. a path
_____ 6. to fire a weapon
_____ 7. a method
_____ 8. something simple, without adornment; clear/evident
_____ 9. to moan in a high pitched voice
_____ 10. an aircraft; a geometric concept of two dimensions
_____ 11. form of ride, past tense
_____ 12. part of something or a group
_____ 13. a mineral deposit
_____ 14. bad smelling; outside the margins
_____ 15. an alcoholic beverage typically made from grapes or berries
_____ 16. to be told what you owe, past tense
_____ 17. a slope to drop things down
_____ 18. to lend something to another
_____ 19. to cut down something (like grass), past tense
_____ 20. a solitary being
_____ 21. move a boat through water using an oar, past tense

142

HOMONYMS 221-230, PUZZLE 3

Use the clues to find the answers in the crossword puzzle.

ACROSS

3 to fire a weapon
4 a path
6 bad smelling; outside the margins
7 to moan in a high pitched voice
9 to fill something. weight/cargo
11 to be told what you owe, past tense
13 a method
14 form of ride, past tense
15 an aircraft; a geometric concept of two dimensions
16 to lend something to another

DOWN

1 a slope to drop things down
2 to cut down something (like grass), past tense
4 move a boat through water using an oar, past tense
5 to construct
6 poultry
8 an alcoholic beverage typically made from grapes or berries
10 part of something or a group
12 a mineral deposit
15 something simple, without adornment; clear/evident
16 a solitary being

HOMONYMS 221-230, PUZZLE 4

Use the clues to find the answers in the word search puzzle. Words can be found horizontally, vertically, or diagonally.

```
R  P  X  D  E  L  L  I  B  D  L  P
D  E  N  I  W  D  P  W  T  W  B  L
S  J  V  H  Q  D  L  O  A  D  W  W
X  O  I  N  I  A  L  P  L  O  X  J
N  N  M  M  K  E  N  I  F  O  E  X
E  E  R  E  M  A  N  M  U  D  N  M
P  T  K  P  O  D  N  A  O  B  O  E
Y  U  L  L  D  A  C  R  L  W  M  S
T  H  L  U  E  O  F  P  E  P  K  U
P  C  V  O  M  R  V  D  Z  K  W  M
M  M  W  F  D  L  N  G  Q  F  X  J
S  H  O  O  T  E  G  R  O  W  E  D
```

_____ 1. total
_____ 2. a path
_____ 3. to fill something. weight/cargo
_____ 4. poultry
_____ 5. to construct
_____ 6. to fire a weapon
_____ 7. an alcoholic beverage typically made from grapes or berries
_____ 8. a method
_____ 9. something simple, without adornment; clear/evident
_____ 10. to moan in a high pitched voice
_____ 11. an aircraft; a geometric concept of two dimensions
_____ 12. form of ride, past tense
_____ 13. part of something or a group
_____ 14. bad smelling; outside the margins
_____ 15. move a boat through water using an oar, past tense
_____ 16. to be told what you owe, past tense
_____ 17. a slope to drop things down
_____ 18. to lend something to another
_____ 19. to cut down something (like grass), past tense
_____ 20. a solitary being
_____ 21. a mineral deposit

144

LESSON 24: HOMONYMS 231 - 240

231.	Morning: Mourning:	The first several hours after the sun comes up. To express grief over something.
232.	Pleas: Please:	Requests. Short for "if you please." To make someone happy.
233.	Roe: Row:	Fish eggs. To put oars in the water and pull in order to propel a boat.
234.	Son: Sun:	Male offspring. A star around which planets rotate.
235.	Whirled: World:	To spin, past tense. A planet.
236.	Bite: Byte:	To sink teeth into something. A computer term for eight bits of information.
237.	Cite: Sight: Site:	To quote or name someone who gave the author information. Vision. A place.
238.	Lore: Lower:	A tale or story. Below something. (Near homonym.)
239.	Muscle: Mussel:	The body tissue that covers the skeleton. An invertebrate water creature that some people eat.
240.	Plum: Plumb:	A small, round purple fruit. A weight attached to a line. Exactly or completely.

Assignment Schedule for One-Year Course

Monday:	Give students the list above. Have them copy Groups 231-233 into their spelling notebook.
Tuesday:	Have students copy Groups 234-236 into their spelling notebook. Do Puzzle 1.
Wednesday:	Have students copy Groups 237-238 into their spelling notebook. Do Puzzle 2.
Thursday:	Have students copy Groups 239-240 into their spelling notebook. Do Puzzle 3.
Friday:	Do Puzzle 4 – without the lesson sheet or spelling notebook.
Friday fun:	Write a paragraph about this wonderful world on which we live. As always, use as many homonyms as you can.

Assignment Schedule for Two-Year Course

Monday:	Give students the list above. Have them copy Groups 231-232 into their spelling notebook.
Tuesday:	Have students copy Groups 233-234 into their spelling notebook.
Wednesday:	Have students copy Groups 235-236 into their spelling notebook.
Thursday:	Have students copy Groups 237-238 into their spelling notebook.
Friday:	Have students copy Groups 239-240 into their spelling notebook.
Monday:	Do Puzzle 1.
Tuesday:	Do Puzzle 2.
Wednesday:	Do Puzzle 3.
Thursday:	Do Puzzle 4. – without the lesson sheet or spelling notebook.
Friday fun:	Write a paragraph about this wonderful world on which we live. As always, use as many homonyms as you can.

HOMONYMS 231-240, PUZZLE 1

Use the clues to find the answers in the crossword puzzle.

ACROSS

3 below something
9 to spin, past tense
10 fish eggs
13 a tale or story
14 the first several hours after the sun comes up
15 a place
17 an invertebrate water creature that some people eat
19 to sink teeth into something
20 a star around which planets rotate
21 the body tissue that covers the skeleton

DOWN

1 a computer term for eight bits of information
2 a planet
4 to put oars in the water and pull in order to propel a boat
5 to express grief over something
6 make someone happy
7 to quote or name someone who gave the author information
8 a weight attached to a line. exactly or completely
11 requests
12 vision
16 a small, round purple fruit
18 male offspring

147

HOMONYMS 231-240, PUZZLE 2

Use the clues to find the answers in the word search puzzle. Words can be found horizontally, vertically, or diagonally.

```
M   U   S   C   L   E   G   N   L   T   R   D
P   L   E   A   S   R   N   B   K   R   B   E
M   N   K   P   O   X   I   L   Y   W   V   L
R   U   U   W   C   X   N   G   R   T   R   R
R   J   S   S   I   X   R   L   T   G   E   I
T   P   D   S   T   L   O   Q   N   M   W   H
R   H   L   X   E   D   M   I   U   S   O   W
O   V   T   E   L   L   N   L   I   D   L   F
E   M   D   R   A   R   P   G   E   T   I   S
G   R   O   C   U   S   H   T   L   W   K   B
Z   W   O   O   F   T   E   B   I   T   E   Q
B   M   M   L   N   O   S   B   M   U   L   P
```

_____ 1. requests
_____ 2. to express grief over something
_____ 3. fish eggs
_____ 4. vision
_____ 5. male offspring
_____ 6. a tale or story
_____ 7. to sink teeth into something
_____ 8. to spin, past tense
_____ 9. a star around which planets rotate
_____ 10. a place
_____ 11. a planet
_____ 12. a computer term for eight bits of information
_____ 13. an invertebrate water creature that some people eat
_____ 14. to quote or name someone who gave the author information
_____ 15. to put oars in the water and pull in order to propel a boat
_____ 16. below something
_____ 17. the body tissue that covers the skeleton
_____ 18. make someone happy
_____ 19. a small, round purple fruit
_____ 20. the first several hours after the sun comes up
_____ 21. a weight attached to a line. exactly or completely

148   Made with 1-2-3 Word Search Maker

HOMONYMS 231-240, PUZZLE 3

Use the clues to find the answers in the crossword puzzle.

ACROSS

2 a tale or story

3 to put oars in the water and pull in order to propel a boat

4 male offspring

9 a small, round purple fruit

11 the first several hours after the sun comes up

12 fish eggs

14 a place

15 to spin, past tense

16 a computer term for eight bits of information

18 to sink teeth into something

20 the body tissue that covers the skeleton

DOWN

1 to express grief over something

5 a planet

6 requests

7 below something

8 vision

9 a weight attached to a line. exactly or completely

10 an invertebrate water creature that some people eat

13 make someone happy

17 to quote or name someone who gave the author information

19 a star around which planets rotate

HOMONYMS 231-240, PUZZLE 4

Use the clues to find the answers in the word search puzzle. Words can be found horizontally, vertically, or diagonally.

```
E  P  L  U  M  B  P  L  E  A  S  C
L  N  P  N  R  W  N  O  S  G  E  D
C  R  U  L  K  E  V  L  N  B  R  E
S  G  M  S  E  L  W  I  L  D  O  L
U  N  R  F  V  A  N  O  R  D  L  R
M  I  T  T  R  R  S  B  L  C  S  I
L  N  D  O  U  M  R  E  Y  I  G  H
N  R  W  O  T  D  O  Q  G  T  B  W
R  O  M  L  L  M  E  H  T  E  E  Z
Z  M  K  R  U  L  T  E  T  I  S  F
Q  N  O  L  J  L  E  S  S  U  M  H
J  W  P  N  B  I  T  E  N  R  Z  H
```

_____ 1. a place
_____ 2. to express grief over something
_____ 3. fish eggs
_____ 4. below something
_____ 5. male offspring
_____ 6. a tale or story
_____ 7. to sink teeth into something
_____ 8. to spin, past tense
_____ 9. a star around which planets rotate
_____ 10. vision
_____ 11. a planet
_____ 12. a computer term for eight bits of information
_____ 13. a small, round purple fruit
_____ 14. to quote or name someone who gave the author information
_____ 15. to put oars in the water and pull in order to propel a boat
_____ 16. requests
_____ 17. the body tissue that covers the skeleton
_____ 18. make someone happy
_____ 19. an invertebrate water creature that some people eat
_____ 20. the first several hours after the sun comes up
_____ 21. a weight attached to a line. exactly or completely

LESSON 25: HOMONYMS 241 - 250

241.	Roil: Royal:	To stir up. Someone/thing related to the ruling family of a country.
242.	Sot: Sought:	A drunk or alcoholic. To look for, past tense.
243.	Woman: Women:	One female human. Two or more females. *Near homonyms; often confused.*
244.	Blew: Blue:	To blow air, past tense. A color associated with the sky.
245.	Clause: Claws:	A group of words containing a subject and a verb. A portion of a legal document. Sharp extensions from the end of an animal's paws.
246.	Mustard: Mustered:	A spicy, yellow condiment. To bring together a group of soldiers, past tense.
247.	Pole: Poll:	A long thin, round stick. A place to vote.
248.	Role: Roll:	A job description. A set of expected behaviors. A list; in school, the students in a class.
249.	Sough: Sue:	When the wind makes a sighing or moaning sound. To take someone to court for payment of a debt or to right a wrong.
250.	Wood: Would:	The trunk of a tree. Helping verb indicating that something can be done.

Assignment Schedule for One-Year Course

Monday:	Give students the list above. Have them copy Groups 241-243 into their spelling notebook..
Tuesday:	Have students copy Groups 244-246 into their spelling notebook. Do Puzzle 1.
Wednesday:	Have students copy Groups 247-248 into their spelling notebook. Do Puzzle 2.
Thursday:	Have students copy Groups 249-250 into their spelling notebook. Do Puzzle 3.
Friday:	Do Puzzle 4 – without the lesson sheet or spelling notebook.
Friday fun:	Write a fable about an animal with claws. Remember to use as many homonyms as you can.

Assignment Schedule for Two-Year Course

Monday:	Give students the list above. Have them copy Groups 241-242 into their spelling notebook.
Tuesday:	Have students copy Groups 243-244 into their spelling notebook.
Wednesday:	Have students copy Groups 245-246 into their spelling notebook.
Thursday:	Have students copy Groups 247-248 into their spelling notebook.
Friday:	Have students copy Groups 249-250 into their spelling notebook.
Monday:	Do Puzzle 1.
Tuesday:	Do Puzzle 2.
Wednesday:	Do Puzzle 3.
Thursday:	Do Puzzle 4. – without the lesson sheet or spelling notebook.
Friday fun:	Write a fable about an animal with claws. Remember to use as many homonyms as you can.

HOMONYMS 241-250, PUZZLE 1

Use the clues to find the answers in the crossword puzzle.

ACROSS

1 a spicy, yellow condiment
3 two or more females
7 a list; in school, the students in a class
8 to blow air, past tense
10 a long thin, round stick
11 a place to vote
12 a job description. a set of expected behaviors
13 a group of words containing a subject and a verb
14 the trunk of a tree
15 when the wind makes a sighing or moaning sound
16 to look for, past tense

DOWN

2 to stir up
4 to bring together a group of soldiers, past tense
5 to take someone to court for payment of a debt or to right a wrong
6 someone/thing related to the ruling family of a country
8 a color associated with the sky
9 one female human
13 sharp extensions from the end of an animal's paws
14 helping verb indicating that something can be done
15 a drunk or alcoholic

HOMONYMS 241-250, PUZZLE 2

Use the clues to find the answers in the word search puzzle. Words can be found horizontally, vertically, or diagonally.

```
K  W  O  O  D  B  L  Q  K  E  J  R
B  Z  E  B  R  A  L  B  U  R  W  N
D  H  T  U  Y  H  K  S  O  T  J  X
E  W  G  O  L  M  U  S  T  A  R  D
R  O  R  U  T  B  L  Q  K  C  F  M
E  M  Y  E  O  S  D  W  E  L  B  P
T  A  W  S  L  S  O  Z  P  R  P  W
S  N  O  U  I  K  K  U  S  O  O  Z
U  P  U  A  O  N  R  W  G  M  L  R
M  P  L  L  R  O  A  Y  E  H  L  E
K  K  D  C  L  L  L  N  V  K  T  V
N  L  R  E  C  K  Q  L  L  O  R  L
```

_____ 1. to stir up
_____ 2. a drunk or alcoholic
_____ 3. a place to vote
_____ 4. one female human
_____ 5. a list; in school, the students in a class
_____ 6. to blow air, past tense
_____ 7. a color associated with the sky
_____ 8. sharp extensions from the end of an animal's paws
_____ 9. a spicy, yellow condiment
_____ 10. two or more females
_____ 11. a long thin, round stick
_____ 12. to look for, past tense
_____ 13. a job description. a set of expected behaviors
_____ 14. when the wind makes a sighing or moaning sound
_____ 15. someone/thing related to the ruling family of a country
_____ 16. the trunk of a tree
_____ 17. bring together a group of soldiers, past tense
_____ 18. to take someone to court for payment of a debt or to right a wrong
_____ 19. helping verb indicating that something can be done
_____ 20. a group of words containing a subject and a verb

HOMONYMS 241-250, PUZZLE 3

Use the clues to find the answers in the crossword puzzle.

ACROSS

4 a place to vote
5 helping verb indicating that something can be done
6 a color associated with the sky
7 to take someone to court for payment of a debt or to right a wrong
8 one female human
12 a group of words containing a subject and a verb
14 to look for, past tense
15 a long thin, round stick
16 someone/thing related to the ruling family of a country
17 a job description. a set of expected behaviors
18 the trunk of a tree

DOWN

1 two or more females
2 a drunk or alcoholic
3 sharp extensions from the end of an animal's paws
6 to blow air, past tense
9 to bring together a group of soldiers, past tense
10 when the wind makes a sighing or moaning sound
11 a spicy, yellow condiment
13 to stir up
17 a list; in school, the students in a class

HOMONYMS 241-250, PUZZLE 4

Use the clues to find the answers in the word search puzzle. Words can be found horizontally, vertically, or diagonally.

```
M U S T A R D P E T V P
M C Y E L O R W O U O R
Z F P S L F S L O L L H
Z H R U L W S W L U E B
V C D A A Z O O M O L B
R L Y L N M K M U K R D
J O C C E H N L S G Q K
R Q Q N W G G I T T H X
G S O T O U Y O E X D T
W E L B M O L R R P K E
H M D G A S P G E M U X
W O O D N B K T D S N R
```

_____ 1. to stir up
_____ 2. one female human
_____ 3. to look for, past tense
_____ 4. a list; in school, the students in a class
_____ 5. to blow air, past tense
_____ 6. to take someone to court for payment of a debt or to right a wrong
_____ 7. a color associated with the sky
_____ 8. a place to vote
_____ 9. a spicy, yellow condiment
_____ 10. two or more females
_____ 11. a long thin, round stick
_____ 12. a job description. a set of expected behaviors
_____ 13. when the wind makes a sighing or moaning sound
_____ 14. someone/thing related to the ruling family of a country
_____ 15. a drunk or alcoholic
_____ 16. the trunk of a tree
_____ 17. bring together a group of soldiers, past tense
_____ 18. helping verb indicating that something can be done
_____ 19. sharp extensions from the end of an animal's paws
_____ 20. a group of words containing a subject and a verb

LESSON 26: HOMONYMS 251 - 260

251.	Boar: Bore:	A male wild pig. To drill. To cause a lack of interest or to make weary.
252.	Complement: Compliment:	Balance, accompaniment, add to. To praise or flatter.
253.	Poor: Pore: Pour:	Not having much money. Pitiful. A hole or minute opening. Cause to flow; rain heavily.
254.	Root: Route:	The bottom of a plant. The basic or bottom part of something. A path.
255.	Stair: Stare:	A step(s) leading from one level to another. To look at for a long period of time, typically without blinking.
256.	Board: Bored:	A straight piece of wood. A group of people who manage an organization. Uninterested; tired of something.
257.	Cord: Chord:	String, twine, or rope. Two or more notes used to form one sound.
258.	Praise: Prays: Preys:	To compliment. To request something, typically used in a religious sense. To stalk.
259.	Rote: Wrote:	Memory. To put pen to paper, past tense.
260.	Staff: Staph:	Employees. Short term for staphylococcus, which causes serious infections.

Assignment Schedule for One-Year Course

Monday:	Give students the list above. Have them copy Groups 251-253 into their spelling notebook.
Tuesday:	Have students copy Groups 254-256 into their spelling notebook. Do Puzzle 1.
Wednesday:	Have students copy Groups 257-258 into their spelling notebook. Do Puzzle 2.
Thursday:	Have students copy Groups 259-260 into their spelling notebook. Do Puzzle 3.
Friday:	Do Puzzle 4 – without the lesson sheet or spelling notebook.
Friday fun:	Using these homonyms, write a commercial.

Assignment Schedule for Two-Year Course

Monday:	Give students the list above. Have them copy Groups 251-252 into their spelling notebook.
Tuesday:	Have students copy Groups 253-254 into their spelling notebook.
Wednesday:	Have students copy Groups 255-256 into their spelling notebook.
Thursday:	Have students copy Groups 257-258 into their spelling notebook.
Friday:	Have students copy Groups 259-260 into their spelling notebook.
Monday:	Do Puzzle 1.
Tuesday:	Do Puzzle 2.
Wednesday:	Do Puzzle 3.
Thursday:	Do Puzzle 4. – without the lesson sheet or spelling notebook.
Friday fun:	Using these homonyms, write a commercial.

HOMONYMS 251-260, PUZZLE 1

Use the clues to find the answers in the crossword puzzle.

ACROSS

2 memory
4 cause to flow; rain heavily
5 string, twine, or rope
7 to drill; to cause a lack of interest or to make weary
9 two or more notes used to form one sound
11 to praise or flatter
13 short term for staphylococcus, which causes serious infections
17 to compliment
18 to look at for a long period of time, typically without blinking
19 a male wild pig
20 employees
21 to put pen to paper, past tense

DOWN

1 balance, accompaniment, add to
3 a straight piece of wood; a group of people who manage an organization
6 the bottom of a plant. the basic or bottom part of something
8 uninterested; tired of something
10 a path
12 to stalk
14 to request something, typically used in a religious sense
15 a step(s) leading from one level to another
16 not having much money; pitiful
17 a hole or minute opening

HOMONYMS 251-260, PUZZLE 2

Use the clues to find the answers in the word search puzzle. Words can be found horizontally, vertically, or diagonally.

```
S  C  O  M  P  L  I  M  E  N  T  J
M  Y  H  B  V  P  R  A  Y  S  T  E
F  Y  E  M  O  T  S  T  A  P  H  S
R  P  N  R  L  R  F  F  A  T  S  I
P  C  O  M  P  L  E  M  E  N  T  A
T  O  O  R  E  C  C  D  G  E  J  R
E  R  O  B  O  T  L  B  R  E  B  P
T  I  R  R  P  R  U  O  T  E  O  F
O  A  D  P  O  A  B  O  R  U  A  H
R  T  R  W  R  O  R  A  R  J  R  L
W  S  L  D  E  B  T  P  R  Z  D  Q
N  W  J  N  L  S  D  R  O  H  C  N
```

_____ 1. a male wild pig
_____ 2. a hole or minute opening
_____ 3. employees
_____ 4. to look at for a long period of time without blinking
_____ 5. to praise or flatter
_____ 6. string, twine, or rope
_____ 7. cause to flow; rain heavily
_____ 8. a path
_____ 9. a step(s) leading from one level to another
_____ 10. a straight piece of wood
_____ 11. balance, accompaniment, add to
_____ 12. two or more notes used to form one sound
_____ 13. to compliment
_____ 14. not having much money; pitiful
_____ 15. uninterested; tired of something
_____ 16. to stalk
_____ 17. memory
_____ 18. to put pen to paper, past tense
_____ 19. to drill. to cause a lack of interest or to make weary
_____ 20. to request something, typically used in a religious sense
_____ 21. short term for staphylococcus, which causes serious infections
_____ 22. the bottom of a plant. the basic or bottom part of something.

Made with 1-2-3 Word Search Maker

HOMONYMS 251-260, PUZZLE 3

Use the clues to find the answers in the crossword puzzle.

ACROSS

4 a hole or minute opening
6 two or more notes used to form one sound
9 a path
10 to look at for a long period of time, typically without blinking
11 not having much money; pitiful
12 short term for staphylococcus, which causes serious infections
13 to compliment
17 to praise or flatter
19 a male wild pig
20 the bottom of a plant. the basic or bottom part of something
21 employees

DOWN

1 to drill; to cause a lack of interest or to make weary
2 uninterested; tired of something
3 to request something, typically used in a religious sense
5 cause to flow; rain heavily
6 string, twine, or rope
7 balance, accompaniment, add to
8 to put pen to paper, past tense
14 memory
15 a step(s) leading from one level to another
16 a straight piece of wood; a group of people who manage an organization
18 to stalk

HOMONYMS 251-260, PUZZLE 4

Use the clues to find the answers in the word search puzzle. Words can be found horizontally, vertically, or diagonally.

```
K  D  M  W  R  O  T  E  T  L  P  H  M
F  B  D  C  O  M  P  L  E  M  E  N  T
P  P  C  K  N  C  Y  C  F  F  A  T  S
R  F  E  O  R  G  O  S  T  A  R  E  E
A  J  T  G  M  R  K  R  Q  O  P  R  B
Y  B  U  E  D  P  I  L  N  T  O  H  O
S  K  O  K  S  A  L  D  B  B  O  R  R
K  S  R  R  T  I  X  I  H  O  R  L  E
T  Y  X  S  R  H  A  W  M  H  A  E  D
K  E  B  R  U  O  P  R  P  E  T  R  P
F  R  D  R  O  H  C  A  P  O  N  O  D
F  P  B  T  N  Y  T  O  R  J  R  T  Y
M  L  T  G  R  S  X  B  K  E  M  R  K
```

_____ 1. to stalk
_____ 2. a male wild pig
_____ 3. a path
_____ 4. a hole or minute opening
_____ 5. employees
_____ 6. memory
_____ 7. to praise or flatter
_____ 8. to compliment
_____ 9. string, twine, or rope
_____ 10. cause to flow; rain heavily
_____ 11. a step(s) leading from one level to another
_____ 12. a straight piece of wood
_____ 13. balance, accompaniment, add to
_____ 14. two or more notes used to form one sound
_____ 15. not having much money. pitiful
_____ 16. to look at for a long period of time without blinking
_____ 17. uninterested; tired of something
_____ 18. to put pen to paper, past tense
_____ 19. to drill. to cause a lack of interest or to make weary
_____ 20. short term for staphylococcus, which causes serious infections
_____ 21. the bottom of a plant. the basic or bottom part of something
_____ 22. to request something, typically used in a religious sense

162

LESSON 27: HOMONYMS 261 - 270

261.	Boarder:	One who lives with another and pays part of the expenses.
	Border:	An edge of something, such as a garment or country.
262.	Council:	A group that manages an organization.
	Counsel:	To give advice.
263.	Principal:	The person who runs a school.
	Principle:	An important or guiding point.
264.	Rough:	Not smooth.
	Ruff:	A fancy pleated collar. Neck hair or feathers.
265.	Stalk:	To quietly follow with the intention of doing harm.
	Stock:	Products on hand.
266.	Bode:	To be an indication of something that is about to occur.
	Bowed:	To be bent over, past tense.
267.	Councilor:	A member of a council.
	Counselor:	One who gives advice.
268.	Presence:	The physical existence of someone and something in a particular place.
	Presents:	Gifts.
269.	Rout:	Tumult, disorder, riot. To thoroughly defeat; to trounce.
	Route:	A path.
270.	Steal:	To take without permission.
	Steel:	Very strong metal.

Assignment Schedule for One-Year Course

Monday:	Give students the list above. Have them copy Groups 261-263 into their spelling notebook.
Tuesday:	Have students copy Groups 264-266 into their spelling notebook. Do Puzzle 1.
Wednesday:	Have students copy Groups 267-268 into their spelling notebook. Do Puzzle 2.
Thursday:	Have students copy Groups 269-270 into their spelling notebook. Do Puzzle 3.
Friday:	Do Puzzle 4 – without the lesson sheet or spelling notebook.
Friday fun:	Write a paragraph about your school or home school. Be sure you tell about your principal and counselor.

Assignment Schedule for Two-Year Course

Monday:	Give students the list above. Have them copy Groups 261-262 into their spelling notebook.
Tuesday:	Have students copy Groups 263-264 into their spelling notebook.
Wednesday:	Have students copy Groups 265-266 into their spelling notebook.
Thursday:	Have students copy Groups 267-268 into their spelling notebook.
Friday:	Have students copy Groups 269-270 into their spelling notebook.
Monday:	Do Puzzle 1.
Tuesday:	Do Puzzle 2.
Wednesday:	Do Puzzle 3.
Thursday:	Do Puzzle 4. – without the lesson sheet or spelling notebook.
Friday fun:	Write a paragraph about your school or home school. Be sure you tell about your principal and counselor.

HOMONYMS 261-270, PUZZLE 1

Use the clues to find the answers in the crossword puzzle.

ACROSS

1 to give advice

2 an edge of something, such as a garment or country

4 not smooth

6 to quietly follow with the intention of doing harm

7 products on hand

8 an important or guiding point

11 tumult, disorder, riot; to thoroughly defeat; to trounce

12 to be an indication of something that is about to occur

14 to take without permission

15 a group that manages an organization

16 the physical existence of someone and something in a particular place

DOWN

1 one who gives advice

2 one who lives with another and pays part of the expenses

3 a fancy pleated collar. neck hair or feathers

5 a member of a council

8 gifts

9 the person who runs a school

10 to be bent over, past tense

13 a path

14 very strong metal

HOMONYMS 261-270, PUZZLE 2

Use the clues to find the answers in the word search puzzle. Words can be found horizontally, vertically, or diagonally.

```
N  P  L  A  E  T  S  B  O  D  E  L  F
R  R  B  N  S  T  N  E  S  E  R  P  R
O  I  K  R  F  D  M  T  P  E  F  O  S
L  N  K  E  K  F  C  X  D  J  L  T  P
I  C  R  D  C  N  U  R  L  E  E  R  K
C  I  K  R  R  O  O  R  S  E  I  C  R
N  P  L  A  O  B  U  N  L  N  O  O  Z
U  A  A  O  U  B  U  N  C  T  U  Z  Q
O  L  T  B  T  O  O  I  S  T  D  C  Q
C  R  S  J  C  H  P  W  E  E  L  D  V
H  L  D  M  Y  L  N  F  E  L  L  C  W
P  R  E  S  E  N  C  E  F  D  T  M  M
M  H  G  U  O  R  C  O  U  N  C  I  L
```

_____ 1. not smooth

_____ 2. an edge of something, such as a garment or country

_____ 3. a group that manages an organization

_____ 4. products on hand

_____ 5. a path

_____ 6. the person who runs a school

_____ 7. gifts

_____ 8. one who gives advice

_____ 9. to take without permission

_____ 10. an important or guiding point

_____ 11. a fancy pleated collar. neck hair or feathers

_____ 12. to quietly follow with the intention of doing harm

_____ 13. to be an indication of something that is about to occur

_____ 14. to be bent over, past tense

_____ 15. to give advice

_____ 16. one who lives with another and pays part of the expenses

_____ 17. very strong metal

_____ 18. a member of a council

_____ 19. the physical existence of someone in a particular place

_____ 20. tumult, disorder, riot; to thoroughly defeat; to trounce

Made with Crossword Weaver

HOMONYMS 261-270, PUZZLE 3

Use the clues to find the answers in the crossword puzzle.

ACROSS

- **3** a member of a council
- **8** the person who runs a school
- **9** to give advice
- **12** one who gives advice
- **13** to be an indication of something that is about to occur
- **14** gifts
- **17** a path
- **18** not smooth
- **19** very strong metal

DOWN

- **1** a fancy pleated collar. neck hair or feathers
- **2** a group that manages an organization
- **4** to take without permission
- **5** an important or guiding point
- **6** products on hand
- **7** the physical existence of someone and something in a particular place
- **10** to be bent over, past tense
- **11** one who lives with another and pays part of the expenses
- **13** an edge of something, such as a garment or country
- **15** to quietly follow with the intention of doing harm
- **16** tumult, disorder, riot; to thoroughly defeat; to trounce

HOMONYMS 261-270, PUZZLE 4

Use the clues to find the answers in the word search puzzle. Words can be found horizontally, vertically, or diagonally.

```
H  G  U  O  R  P  W  F  M  B  Y  V  P  T  T
B  H  R  K  D  M  G  K  F  L  O  R  L  K  P
N  P  X  V  K  C  L  X  F  U  I  W  C  D  R
M  G  J  B  L  T  O  C  L  N  R  O  E  X  I
T  C  K  B  A  B  H  U  C  L  T  B  F  D  N
T  O  W  C  T  L  C  I  N  S  M  P  G  T  C
R  U  N  O  S  K  P  T  Q  S  B  O  D  E  I
T  N  J  U  W  L  K  S  T  N  E  S  E  R  P
B  S  R  N  E  H  W  S  T  E  E  L  K  R  A
J  E  E  C  T  C  O  U  N  C  I  L  E  R  L
R  L  D  I  L  U  T  J  Y  F  A  S  E  G  E
R  O  R  L  K  B  O  K  N  E  E  D  Q  D  T
C  R  A  O  Y  L  J  R  T  N  R  Z  L  K  U
M  X  O  R  R  G  Y  S  C  O  L  K  W  X  O
W  Y  B  B  R  D  N  E  B  M  M  N  T  X  R
```

_____ 1. not smooth
_____ 2. gifts
_____ 3. a group that manages an organization
_____ 4. products on hand
_____ 5. a path
_____ 6. the person who runs a school
_____ 7. to give advice
_____ 8. to take without permission
_____ 9. an important or guiding point
_____ 10. the physical existence of something in a particular place
_____ 11. an edge of something, such as a garment or country
_____ 12. a fancy pleated collar. neck hair or feathers
_____ 13. to be an indication of something that is about to occur
_____ 14. to be bent over, past tense
_____ 15. one who lives with another and pays part of the expenses
_____ 16. one who gives advice
_____ 17. to quietly follow with the intention of doing harm
_____ 18. very strong metal
_____ 19. a member of a council
_____ 20. tumult, disorder, riot; to thoroughly defeat; to trounce

168

LESSON 28: HOMONYMS 271 - 280

271.	Born: Borne:	To be brought into this world. To bear, past tense.
272.	Creak: Creek:	To make a squeaky sound, usually involving wood. A small body of running, fresh water; smaller than a river.
273.	Pros: Prose:	Short form of the word professionals. Non-poetic writing.
274.	Rung: Wrung:	A step on a ladder. To sound a bell, past tense. To squeeze liquid from cloth by twisting it, past tense.
275.	Stile: Style:	Steps for climbing over a fence. Fashion or method.
276.	Borough: Burro: Burrow:	A division of New York City. A small donkey. A small tunnel in the ground, made by animals for shelter.
277.	Straight: Strait:	In a direct line. A narrow body of water, often between cliffs.
278.	Bough: Bow:	A large limb on a tree. To bend at the waist to show respect.
279.	Brake: Break:	To stop. Device used to stop. To cause something to no longer work. A brief respite.
280.	Breaches: Breeches:	A break in a wall. An old name for pants. *Near homonym.*

Assignment Schedule for One-Year Course

Monday:	Give students the list above. Have them copy Groups 271-273 into their spelling notebook.
Tuesday:	Have students copy Groups 274-276 into their spelling notebook. Do Puzzle 1.
Wednesday:	Have students copy Groups 277-278 into their spelling notebook. Do Puzzle 2.
Thursday:	Have students copy Groups 279-280 into their spelling notebook. Do Puzzle 3.
Friday:	Do Puzzle 4 – without the lesson sheet or spelling notebook.
Friday fun:	Write a fable about a burro; be sure to use as many homonyms as you can.

Assignment Schedule for Two-Year Course

Monday:	Give students the list above. Have them copy Groups 271-272 into their spelling notebook.
Tuesday:	Have students copy Groups 273-274 into their spelling notebook.
Wednesday:	Have students copy Groups 275-276 into their spelling notebook.
Thursday:	Have students copy Groups 277-278 into their spelling notebook.
Friday:	Have students copy Groups 279-280 into their spelling notebook.
Monday:	Do Puzzle 1.
Tuesday:	Do Puzzle 2.
Wednesday:	Do Puzzle 3.
Thursday:	Do Puzzle 4. – without the lesson sheet or spelling notebook.
Friday fun:	Write a fable about a burro; be sure to use as many homonyms as you can.

HOMONYMS 271-280, PUZZLE 1

Use the clues to find the answers in the crossword puzzle.

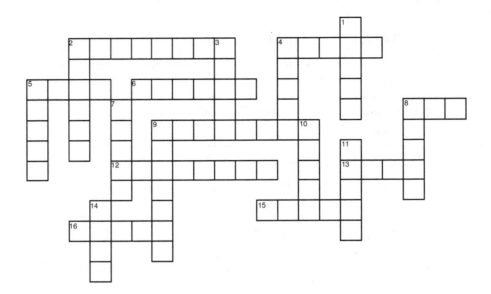

ACROSS

- **2** a break in a wall
- **4** a small donkey
- **5** to be brought into this world
- **6** a narrow body of water, often between cliffs
- **8** to bend at the waist to show respect
- **9** an old name for pants
- **12** in a direct line
- **13** a step on a ladder. to sound a bell, past tense
- **15** a small body of running, fresh water; smaller than a river
- **16** to squeeze liquid from cloth by twisting it, past tense

DOWN

- **1** to make a squeaky sound, usually involving wood
- **2** a small tunnel in the ground, made by animals for shelter
- **3** steps for climbing over a fence
- **4** to bear, past tense
- **5** to cause something to no longer work. a brief respite
- **7** non-poetic writing
- **8** a large limb on a tree
- **9** a division of New York City
- **10** fashion or method
- **11** to stop; device used to stop
- **14** short form of the word professionals

171

HOMONYMS 271-280, PUZZLE 2

Use the clues to find the answers in the word search puzzle. Words can be found horizontally, vertically, or diagonally.

```
P  X  X  G  C  R  E  A  K  P  X  E  M
M  W  B  R  E  A  K  C  R  W  K  R  S
H  B  O  L  J  W  K  O  R  A  R  T  L
F  R  Y  B  E  B  S  V  R  E  R  T  E
G  T  T  R  L  E  R  B  F  A  E  N  M
S  N  B  R  I  B  B  E  I  W  R  K  T
K  M  U  X  T  R  R  G  E  O  D  F  I
R  P  R  R  S  J  H  E  B  C  P  Q  A
N  R  R  R  W  T  B  K  A  T  H  L  R
K  O  O  N  G  N  U  R  C  Q  E  T
Y  S  W  M  R  Q  Q  J  R  M  H  M  S
D  B  O  R  O  U  G  H  K  R  K  E  M
D  N  X  L  B  N  G  H  G  U  O  B  S
```

_____ 1. to bear, past tense
_____ 2, to make a squeaky sound, usually involving wood
_____ 3. non-poetic writing
_____ 4. a large limb on a tree
_____ 5. to stop; device used to stop
_____ 6. a break in a wall
_____ 7. a step on a ladder. to sound a bell, past tense
_____ 8. fashion or method
_____ 9. a division of New York City
_____ 10. a small donkey
_____ 11. short form of the word professionals
_____ 12. in a direct line
_____ 13. to be brought into this world
_____ 14. to bend at the waist to show respect
_____ 15. a small tunnel in the ground, made by animals for shelter
_____ 16. a narrow body of water, often between cliffs
_____ 17. steps for climbing over a fence
_____ 18. to cause something to no longer work. a brief respite
_____ 19. a small body of running, fresh water; smaller than a river
_____ 20. an old name for pants
_____ 21. to squeeze liquid from cloth by twisting it, past tense

172   Made with Crossword Weaver

HOMONYMS 271-280, PUZZLE 3

Use the clues to find the answers in the crossword puzzle.

ACROSS

2 to be brought into this world
4 a small donkey
5 to bend at the waist to show respect
6 fashion or method
7 to cause something to no longer work. a brief respite
10 a break in a wall
12 to bear, past tense
16 in a direct line
17 to make a squeaky sound, usually involving wood

DOWN

1 a step on a ladder. to sound a bell, past tense
2 a division of New York City
3 non-poetic writing
4 an old name for pants
5 to stop; device used to stop
8 to squeeze liquid from cloth by twisting it, past tense
9 a small tunnel in the ground, made by animals for shelter
11 a narrow body of water, often between cliffs
12 a large limb on a tree
13 short form of the word professionals
14 steps for climbing over a fence
15 a small body of running, fresh water; smaller than a river

173

HOMONYMS 271-280, PUZZLE 4

Use the clues to find the answers in the word search puzzle. Words can be found horizontally, vertically, or diagonally.

```
C  N  K  F  B  R  E  A  K  F  B  N  X  G
T  R  G  L  L  Y  Z  W  Q  P  U  M  F  E
H  Y  E  N  S  E  H  C  E  E  R  B  N  Z
D  L  B  E  U  R  T  R  L  Q  R  R  T  S
C  L  M  U  K  R  V  W  I  C  O  N  T  H
S  G  N  U  R  P  W  M  T  B  W  R  R  Q
E  Y  V  R  R  N  Z  S  Z  A  O  T  R
H  C  Z  O  P  C  O  H  F  I  E  B  K  B
C  Z  S  W  E  J  J  F  G  L  V  F  B  Y
A  E  D  K  P  R  T  H  Y  U  D  M  P  W
E  Z  A  P  J  L  T  T  L  J  O  R  R  O
R  R  W  L  L  N  S  J  T  H  N  B  O  B
B  T  I  A  R  T  S  W  M  L  K  Z  S  L
B  O  R  O  U  G  H  C  R  E  A  K  K  N
```

_____ 1. to bear, past tense
_____ 2. in a direct line
_____ 3. non-poetic writing
_____ 4. a large limb on a tree
_____ 5. to stop; device used to stop
_____ 6. a break in a wall
_____ 7. to bend at the waist to show respect
_____ 8. a small body of running, fresh water; smaller than a river
_____ 9. fashion or method
_____ 10. a division of New York City
_____ 11. a small donkey
_____ 12. short form of the word professionals
_____ 13. to be brought into this world
_____ 14. a small tunnel in the ground, made by animals for shelter
_____ 15. a narrow body of water, often between cliffs
_____ 16. a step on a ladder. to sound a bell, past tense
_____ 17. to make a squeaky sound, usually involving wood
_____ 18. steps for climbing over a fence
_____ 19. to cause something to no longer work. a brief respite
_____ 20. an old name for pants
_____ 21. to squeeze liquid from cloth by twisting it, past tense

LESSON 29: HOMONYMS 281 - 290

281.	Bread:	The baked good we make sandwiches on.
	Bred:	To raise or produce, past tense. Type or kind.
282.	Bridal:	Having to do with a bride.
	Bridle:	A harness used to control a large animal.
283.	Buy:	To purchase.
	By:	Preposition that shows the means or a preposition meaning near.
	Bye:	Farewell.
284.	Coo:	A soft sound made by a dove.
	Coup:	A successful stroke or act.
285.	Coop:	A small building where chickens are kept.
	Coupe:	A small two-door car that seats two people.
286.	Core:	The center of an object.
	Corps:	An organized group of people working together.
287.	Finish:	To complete something.
	Finnish:	Something from Finland.
288.	Serge:	To bind the edges of fabric (as with a serger).
	Surge:	To move ahead quickly.
289.	Suite:	A set of rooms or matching furniture. A set of instrumental works played together.
	Sweat:	Perspiration. *Near homonym.*
	Sweet:	Pleasant. Tasty or kind.
290.	Whoa:	An exclamation to stop.
	Woe:	An old word for sorrow or despair.

Assignment Schedule for One-Year Course

Monday:	Give students the list above. Have them copy Groups 281-283 into their spelling notebook.
Tuesday:	Have students copy Groups 284-286 into their spelling notebook. Do Puzzle 1.
Wednesday:	Have students copy Groups 287-288 into their spelling notebook. Do Puzzle 2.
Thursday:	Have students copy Groups 289-290 into their spelling notebook. Do Puzzle 3.
Friday:	Do Puzzle 4 – without the lesson sheet or spelling notebook.
Friday fun:	Write a paragraph about wedding plans. Use as many homonyms as you can.

Assignment Schedule for Two-Year Course

Monday:	Give students the list above. Have them copy Groups 281-282 into their spelling notebook.
Tuesday:	Have students copy Groups 283-284 into their spelling notebook.
Wednesday:	Have students copy Groups 285-286 into their spelling notebook.
Thursday:	Have students copy Groups 287-288 into their spelling notebook.
Friday:	Have students copy Groups 289-290 into their spelling notebook.
Monday:	Do Puzzle 1.
Tuesday:	Do Puzzle 2.
Wednesday:	Do Puzzle 3.
Thursday:	Do Puzzle 4. – without the lesson sheet or spelling notebook.
Friday fun:	Write a paragraph about wedding plans. Use as many homonyms as you can.

Write a paragraph about wedding plans. Use as many homonyms as you can.

HOMONYMS 281-290, PUZZLE 1

Use the clues to find the answers in the crossword puzzle.

ACROSS

1 farewell
2 preposition that shows the means or a preposition meaning near
3 an organized group of people working together
5 an exclamation to stop
8 a successful stroke or act
9 pleasant. tasty or kind
11 a harness used to control a large animal
12 something from Finland
14 the center of an object
15 the baked good we make sandwiches on
16 a soft sound made by a dove
17 to bind the edges of fabric (as with a serger)

DOWN

1 to purchase
2 having to do with a bride
4 perspiration
6 a small two-door car that seats two people
7 an old word for sorrow or despair
9 a set of rooms or matching furniture
10 to complete something
11 to raise or produce, past tense. type or kind
13 to move ahead quickly
14 a small building where chickens are kept

HOMONYMS 281-290, PUZZLE 2

Use the clues to find the answers in the word search puzzle. Words can be found horizontally, vertically, or diagonally.

```
G D E Y B B G S W E E T
Y A F I N N I S H P K S
C E B R I D A L X P E W
H R H S I N I F O R D E
M B V W P B D O G P B A
E R J Q D U C E C U A T
T C R B H Y O T F O · P Q
I O O M R E M O H C R B
U R Q R D I G W C W Y Q
S P T E E N D R R K O J
X S R D Z W V L U Z R E
K B L T C O U P E S R K
```

_____ 1. to purchase
_____ 2. perspiration
_____ 3. the baked good we make sandwiches on
_____ 4. a successful stroke or act
_____ 5. to complete something
_____ 6. a small building where chickens are kept
_____ 7. having to do with a bride
_____ 8. farewell
_____ 9. a soft sound made by a dove
_____ 10. the center of an object
_____ 11. something from Finland
_____ 12. to move ahead quickly
_____ 13. to raise or produce, past tense. type or kind
_____ 14. an exclamation to stop
_____ 15. a harness used to control a large animal
_____ 16. a small two-door car that seats two people
_____ 17. to bind the edges of fabric (as with a serger)
_____ 18. an organized group of people working together
_____ 19. a set of rooms or matching furniture
_____ 20. an old word for despair
_____ 21. pleasant. tasty or kind
_____ 22. preposition that shows the means or a preposition meaning near

178   Made with Crossword Weaver

HOMONYMS 281-290, PUZZLE 3

Use the clues to find the answers in the crossword puzzle.

ACROSS

1 farewell
2 to purchase
4 to complete something
6 an exclamation to stop
7 the baked good we make sandwiches on
8 a soft sound made by a dove
9 perspiration
10 a small two-door car that seats two people
11 the center of an object
12 pleasant. tasty or kind
14 a harness used to control a large animal
15 something from Finland

DOWN

1 preposition that shows the means or a preposition meaning near
2 having to do with a bride
3 to raise or produce, past tense. type or kind
5 to bind the edges of fabric (as with a serger)
6 an old word for sorrow or despair
8 a successful stroke or act
9 to move ahead quickly
10 a small building where chickens are kept
12 a set of rooms or matching furniture
13 an organized group of people working together

HOMONYMS 281-289, PUZZLE 4

Use the clues to find the answers in the word search puzzle. Words can be found horizontally, vertically, or diagonally.

```
P  B  E  G  R  U  S  S  D  T  S  T
U  J  H  R  R  G  R  E  W  E  A  P
O  B  H  C  T  L  R  T  R  E  O  X
C  J  R  S  O  B  J  G  W  O  E  P
K  C  W  I  I  R  E  S  C  B  D  T
Z  O  V  W  D  N  E  K  Y  E  A  F
E  R  O  H  F  L  N  R  Q  T  E  G
T  P  H  O  X  V  E  I  J  I  R  B
L  S  M  A  C  N  C  H  F  U  B  U
R  Q  R  D  L  F  I  N  I  S  H  Y
E  Y  B  N  B  R  I  D  A  L  M  P
L  C  O  U  P  E  P  V  N  Y  M  M
```

_____ 1. to purchase
_____ 2. perspiration
_____ 3. farewell
_____ 4. a successful stroke or act
_____ 5. to complete something
_____ 6. a small building where chickens are kept
_____ 7. an organized group of people working together
_____ 8. a set of rooms or matching furniture
_____ 9. an old word for sorrow or despair
_____ 10. pleasant. tasty or kind
_____ 11. having to do with a bride
_____ 12. a soft sound made by a dove
_____ 13. the center of an object
_____ 14. something from Finland
_____ 15. to move ahead quickly
_____ 16. to raise or produce, past tense. type or kind
_____ 17. an exclamation to stop
_____ 18. a harness used to control a large animal
_____ 19. the baked good we make sandwiches on
_____ 20. a small two-door car that seats two people
_____ 21. to bind the edges of fabric (as with a serger)
_____ 22. preposition that shows the means or a preposition meaning near

180

HOMONYMS AND NEAR HOMONYMS
Alphabetical Order

1.	A lot: Allot: Alot:	Many. To set aside for someone's use. NEVER, EVER correct
2.	Accept: Except:	Allow or agree to (match up the "A" with agree). To take away (match up the "ex" with excuse or exit). *Near homonyms.*
3.	Adds: Ads Adz:	To put in, insert. To tally or total up. Slang for advertisements A tool that is similar to an ax.
4.	-Ade: Aid: Aide:	Suffix meaning a sweet, fruity drink. To help. A person who helps.
5.	Affect: Effect:	To influence, shape, or change. Result or outcome. To achieve or cause.
6.	Ail: Ale:	To be ill or sick. To have trouble or pain. An alcoholic beverage made from grain.
7.	Air: Heir:	Atmosphere, space, sky. Successor, inheritor.
8.	Aisle: I'll: Isle:	A walkway or passageway. Contraction of *I* and *will*. A small island.
9.	All: Awl:	Each and every one. A large sewing needle, often used for punching holes in leather.
10.	Allowed: Aloud:	To permit, past tense. Spoken so someone can hear.
11.	Ate: Eight:	To consume, specifically food. Past tense. The number between 7 and 9.
12.	Aught: Ought:	Zero. Should.
13.	Away: Aweigh:	To leave an area. To raise an anchor off the bottom of the sea (or bay).
14.	Aye: Eye: I:	Formal way of saying or voting "yes." Bodily organ used for sight. First person personal pronoun; refers to oneself.

15.	Bail:	Money deposited with the courts to assure that a defendant will appear in court.
	Bale:	A large mound of hay packaged for animal consumption.
16.	Bait:	Something used to lure something else.
	Bate:	To hold back something.
17.	Ball:	A sphere, like a basketball or softball.
	Bawl:	The sound made by a calf.
18.	Band:	Group, crowd. Music group. A strip or belt.
	Banned:	Barred, excluded, expelled. Forbidden, illegal.
19.	Bare:	Without appropriate covering.
	Bear:	A large, furry mammal with fearsome claws & teeth.
20.	Bar:	To prevent someone or something from passing.
	Barre:	A long horizontal pole that dancers use for stretching.
21.	Bases:	Places of safety (such as, military or baseball bases)
	Basis:	The foundation of something.
22.	Be:	To exist.
	Bea:	A woman's name, short for Beatrice or Beatrix.
	Bee:	An insect that makes honey.
23.	Beach:	The sandy place between land and sea.
	Beech:	A type of tree used in making furniture; a shrub.
24.	Beat:	To strike something; to win.
	Beet:	A red vegetable with a high sugar content.
25.	Beau:	French for a boyfriend.
	Bow:	A tied ribbon.
26.	Been:	To exist.
	Ben:	A man's name, short for Benjamin.
	Bin:	A box used for storing things.
27.	Beer:	An alcoholic beverage.
	Bier:	A flat surface on which a body is placed.
28.	Berry:	A small fruit that grows on low bushes.
	Bury:	To put in the ground; to hide.
29.	Berth:	A room on a ship or train.
	Birth:	To bring to life.
30.	Better:	A positive description of quality.
	Bettor:	One who places bets.
31.	Billed:	To be told what you owe, past tense.
	Build:	To construct.

32.	Bite: Byte:	To sink teeth into something. A computer term for eight bits of information.
33.	Blew: Blue:	To blow air, past tense. A color associated with the sky.
34.	Boar: Bore:	A male wild pig. To drill. To cause a lack of interest or to make weary.
35.	Board: Bored:	A straight piece of wood. A group of people who manage an organization. Uninterested; tired of something.
36.	Boarder: Border:	One who lives with another and pays part of the expenses. An edge of something, such as a garment or country.
37.	Bode: Bowed:	To be an indication of something that is about to occur. To be bent over, past tense.
38.	Born: Borne:	To be brought into this world. To bear, past tense.
39.	Borough: Burro: Burrow:	A division of New York City. A small donkey. A small tunnel in the ground, made by animals for shelter.
40.	Bough: Bow:	A large limb on a tree. To bend at the waist to show respect.
41.	Brake: Break:	To stop. Device used to stop. To cause something to no longer work. A brief respite.
42.	Breaches: Breeches:	A break in a wall. An old name for pants. *Near homonym.*
43.	Bread: Bred:	The baked good we make sandwiches on. To raise or produce, past tense. Type or kind.
44.	Bridal: Bridle:	Having to do with a bride. A harness used to control a large animal.
45.	Buy: By: Bye:	To purchase. Preposition that shows the means or a preposition meaning near. Farewell.
46.	Cache: Cash:	A place to hide valuables. Money.

47.	Callous:	An attitude that is hardened against someone or something.
	Callus:	A hardened, thickened area of skin.
48.	Can't	Contraction for *can* and *not*.
	Cant	Lean to one side.
49.	Canvas:	A heavy fabric.
	Canvass:	To travel around an area asking people for something, usually information.
50.	Capital:	A seat of government.
	Capitol:	A building where the legislature meets.
51.	Carat:	A unit of weight for precious stones.
	Carrot:	A long, orange vegetable.
	Karat:	A unit of weight for gold.
52.	Caster:	Wheels on the bottom of furniture.
	Castor:	An Indian plant oil with healing properties.
53.	Caught:	To catch, past tense.
	Cot:	A small bed, often transportable.
54.	Cawed:	The sound made by a crow, past tense.
	Cod:	A type of fish typically found in northern waters.
55.	Cede:	To yield or concede.
	Seed:	Kernel used to start a new plant; verb meaning to plant/sow.
56	Ceiling:	The upper surface of a room.
	Sealing:	To seal or close something.
57.	Cell:	A small simple room. A small part of a living organism.
	Sell:	To exchange money for goods.
58.	Censor:	A person who monitors public morals and publications.
	Sensor:	Something that registers an activity.
59.	Cent:	A penny.
	Sent:	To send someone/something elsewhere, past tense.
60.	Cents:	More than one penny.
	Scents:	Smells.
	Sense:	Intelligence or one of the five ways living things understand their environment.
	Since:	Because.

61.	Chile:	A country in South America.
	Chili:	A spicy stew made of tomatoes, ground beef, and red beans.
	Chilly:	Cool or cold.
62.	Chute:	A slope to drop things down.
	Shoot:	To fire a weapon.
63.	Cite:	To quote or name someone who gave the author information.
	Sight:	Vision.
	Site:	A place.
64.	Clause:	A group of words containing a subject and a verb. A portion of a legal document.
	Claws:	Sharp extensions from the end of an animal's paws.
65.	Complement:	Balance, accompaniment, add to.
	Compliment:	To praise or flatter.
66.	Coo:	A soft sound made by a dove.
	Coup:	A successful stroke or act.
67.	Coop:	A small building where chickens are kept.
	Coupe:	A small two-door car that seats two people.
68.	Cord:	String, twine, or rope.
	Chord:	Two or more notes used to form one sound.
69.	Core:	The center of an object.
	Corps:	An organized group of people working together.
70.	Council:	A group that manages an organization.
	Counsel:	To give advice.
71.	Councilor:	A member of a council.
	Counselor:	One who gives advice.
72.	Creak:	To make a squeaky sound, usually involving wood.
	Creek:	A small body of running, fresh water; smaller than a river.
73.	Dawn:	Early morning, just as the sun is rising.
	Don:	Old term meaning to put on (as in clothes)
74.	Days:	24-hour periods.
	Daze:	Confuse.
75.	Dear:	Something or someone important to a person.
	Deer:	An antlered mammal. Venison.
76.	Den:	A small communal living area.
	Din:	A great deal of noise.

77.	Desert: Dessert:	To abandon. A dry place with limited vegetation. A sweet food served after the main part of a meal. (Match up the "ss" with "super sweet.")
78.	Dew: Do: Due:	Moisture that accumulates on the ground over night. Verb meaning to accomplish something. Something owed at a particular time.
79.	Die: Dye:	To cease to live. To change the color of something.
80.	Died: Dyed:	To cease to live, past tense. To change the color of something, past tense.
81.	Doe: Dough:	A female deer. Money.
82.	Does: Dose:	A form of the verb *do*. A prescribed amount or quantity. *Near homonym; included because* does *is frequently misspelled.*
83.	Does: Doze:	2 or more female deer. To sleep lightly.
84.	Done: Dun:	To complete, past tense. A brownish gray color.
85.	Dual: Duel:	Two things working together. A fight, typically between two men with pistols or swords (match the "e" with "each other").
86.	Ewe: You:	A female sheep. Second person pronoun (not *me* or *he/she/it*).
87.	Faint: Feint:	Pale, weak. Soft or quiet. Dizzy, woozy. A trick or maneuver.
88.	Fair: Faire: Fare:	Equitable, even-handed. Also, pale or light colored. A festival, with many things happening at once. The cost of transportation.
89.	Fairy: Ferry:	A tiny being who flies and has magical powers. A commuter boat. To transport or carry.
90.	Faun: Fawn:	A mythological creature similar to a satyr. A young deer.
91.	Fawned: Fond:	To show affection in an insincere manner, past tense. To care for something.
92.	Feat: Feet:	An accomplishment. The body part we walk on.
93.	Find: Fined:	To locate something. To be required to pay a fee, past tense.

94.	Finish:	To complete something.
	Finnish:	Something from Finland.
95.	Flair:	Flamboyant use of a talent or thing.
	Flare:	A bright light used to signal distress.
96.	Flea:	An insect that lives on mammals.
	Flee:	To run away.
97	Fleas:	Insects that live on mammals.
	Flees:	Runs away.
	Fleece:	The hair on sheep that is spun into wool. To cheat or swindle.
98.	Flew:	To propel through the air, past tense.
	Flu:	Short form of "influenza," an upper respiratory illness.
	Flue:	Tube or pipe used to convey heat or smoke outside. [Part of the chimney.]
99.	Flour:	Finely ground grain used for baking.
	Flower:	The colorful part of a plant.
100.	For	A preposition meaning in favor of or on behalf of.
	Fore:	The front.
	Four:	The number between 3 and 5.
101.	Foreword:	An introductory part of a book, written by someone other than the author.
	Forward:	Move ahead.
102.	Forth:	Onward, forward. Out in the open, into the world.
	Fourth:	Ordinal number between third and fifth.
103.	Foul:	Bad smelling. Outside the margins, like a foul ball.
	Fowl:	Poultry, such as chicken or turkey. (Match the "w" with wings.)
104.	Gait:	Walk, pace.
	Gate:	The opening in a fence.
105.	Gnu:	Another name for a wildebeest.
	Knew:	To know (be aware of), past tense.
	New:	Something recent; not old.
106.	Gorilla:	Large ape-like mammal.
	Guerilla:	A military-type fighter who is not in an official army.
107.	Grate:	To cut into small, thin strips. The covering over a hole.
	Great:	Excellent or large.
108.	Groan:	A moan.
	Grown:	An adult. To mature toward adulthood.
109.	Guessed:	To form an opinion without knowing for certain, past tense.
	Guest:	One who visits another.

110.	Hail: Hale:	To call out a greeting. Frozen rain. Healthy.
111.	Hair: Hare:	That which grows on the top of one's head. A rabbit.
112.	Half: Halve: Have:	One of two equal parts. To separate something into two equal parts. To possess something. *Half is a near homonym.*
113.	Hardy: Hearty:	Resilient; tough; strong. Vigorous/energetic. Warm/cheerful. Filling/nourishing.
114.	Hart: Heart:	Old term for a deer. The organ that pumps blood. Feelings or emotions.
115.	Hay: Hey:	Cut grass that is used as food for cows and horses. An interjection to call for a person's attention; a greeting.
116.	Heal: Heel:	To make one better. (Match the "a" with "ail.") The back of the foot.
117.	Hear: Here:	A sense that involves the ear. At this spot.
118.	Heard: Herd:	To sense something with the ear, past tense. A large group of one type of animals.
119.	Hi: High:	An interjection; a greeting. Elevated. Opposite of low.
120.	Him: Hymn:	Personal pronoun referring to a male. A song of praise.
121.	Hole: Whole:	A place in which something has been removed. Complete.
122.	Hour: Our:	60 minutes. Possessive pronoun showing ownership by a group including oneself.
123.	Humorous: Humerus:	Something that is funny. The bone in the upper arm.
124.	Idle: Idol:	Lazy; not working. An object that is worshiped.
125.	In: Inn:	A preposition describing a location. A place that rents rooms to travelers.
126.	Instance: Instants:	An example. Plural form of instant, a moment.

127.	It's:	Contraction for *it* and *is*.
	Its:	Possessive pronoun showing ownership by something not human.
128.	Knead:	To manipulate bread dough so it will rise.
	Kneed:	To use the knee, past tense.
	Need:	Something that is necessary.
129.	Knight:	A trusted warrior in medieval Europe.
	Night:	Evening, after sunset.
130.	Knot:	To tie or loop. To tether or secure.
	Not:	An adverb that negates something.
	Naught:	Nothing, zip, zero, nil.
131.	Know:	To have information.
	No:	Opposite of yes.
132.	Knows:	To have information.
	Nose:	The feature in the center of one's face.
133.	Lain:	To lie in a resting position.
	Lane:	A narrow road.
134.	Lair:	A home or den. A hideout/hangout.
	Layer:	One thing placed directly on top of another.
135.	Lay:	To place something on a surface.
	Lei:	A garland of flowers, typically associated with Hawaii.
136.	Lays:	To place something in a resting position.
	Laze:	To take it easy, relax, and do no work.
137.	Leach:	To remove from soil by percolation.
	Leech:	A bloodsucking worm.
138.	Leak:	A slow drip.
	Leek:	A garden herb similar to an onion.
139.	Lean:	To bend, tilt. To rest, prop up. Thin or slender.
	Lien:	A notice of debt that is placed against property (car or home).
140.	Led:	To be the front person escorting another, past tense.
	Lead:	A metal; formerly, the center of a pencil.
141.	Lent:	A period of sacrifice in the Christian faith.
	Lint:	Loose cotton that collects in the corners of pockets.
142.	Lentil:	Edible seed, often thought of as a bean.
	Lintel:	The part of a door frame over the door.
143.	Lessen:	To decrease.
	Lesson:	A concept that is taught.

144.	Let's: Lets:	Contraction of *let* and *us*. Allows.
145.	Liar: Lyre:	One who tells falsehoods. A stringed instrument from ancient Greece.
146.	Lie: Lye:	An untruth or falsehood. A strong substance used in homemade soap.
147.	Links: Lynx:	Connections to other things. Another name for a bobcat.
148.	Load: Lode:	To fill something. Weight/cargo. A mineral deposit.
149.	Loan: Lone:	To lend something to another. A solitary being.
150.	Lore: Lower:	A tale or story. Below something. (Near homonym.)
151.	Made: Maid:	To make, past tense. A woman who works as a housekeeper.
152.	Mail: Male:	Letters, packages. To send or transmit. A man.
153.	Main: Maine: Mane:	Major, most important. Northernmost state on the East Coast. Curls; extra hair found on the head and shoulders of a horse or a male lion.
154.	Maize: Maze:	Corn. A puzzle that an individual walks through. Confusion/muddle.
155.	Mall: Maul:	A large open area or a large place to shop. To mangle something.
156.	Mantel: Mantle:	A shelf over the fireplace. A cloak.
157.	Mare: Mayor:	A female horse. A person who leads/governs a city.
158.	Marry: Mary Merry:	To join in matrimony. A woman's name. Happy.

159.	Meat: Meet:	Animal flesh. To make someone's acquaintance.
160.	Medal: Meddle: Metal:	An award for doing something important. To involve oneself in someone else's affairs. A strong, natural substance like iron or steel.
161.	Mind: Mined:	The body part where our thoughts and memory reside. To obey. To dig in the earth, past tense.
162.	Miner: Minor:	One who mines or digs in the earth. Someone who is underage.
163.	Might: Mite:	An auxiliary (or helping) verb. A tiny, eight-legged insect that carries diseases.
164.	Missal: Missile:	A book that contains all of the church services for a year. Something that is hurled at (or launched toward) an object.
165.	Moat: Mote:	A body of water that surrounds a castle. An old word for a speck.
166.	Mode: Mowed:	A method. To cut down something (like grass), past tense.
167.	Morning: Mourning:	The first several hours after the sun comes up. To express grief over something.
168.	Muscle: Mussel:	The body tissue that covers the skeleton. An invertebrate water creature that some people eat.
169.	Mustard: Mustered:	A spicy, yellow condiment. To bring together a group of soldiers, past tense.
170.	Naval: Navel:	Relating to the navy. Belly button.
171.	None: Nun:	Not any; no one. A religious woman dedicated to her God through a restricted lifestyle.
172	Oar: Or: Ore:	A paddle used to propel a boat. A conjunction indicating a choice between 2 things. Raw mineral dug out of the earth.
173.	One: Won:	Single. To have a victory, past tense.
174.	Ordinance: Ordnance:	Rule or law. Weapons.
175	Paced: Paste:	To walk back and forth, past tense. Glue.

176.	Pail: Pale:	A bucket. Missing some color.
177.	Pain: Pane:	Discomfort. A sheet of glass.
178.	Pair: Pare: Pear:	Two things grouped together. To peel down in thin strips. A bell-shaped fruit.
179.	Passed: Past:	To go by, past tense. Preposition meaning to go by. Something that happened before the present.
180.	Patience: Patients:	An attitude of being long-suffering. Sick people.
181.	Pause: Paws:	To cause a break in the action. The feet of an animal.
182.	Pea: Pee:	A small, round vegetable. The 16th letter of the alphabet.
183.	Peace: Piece:	Calm. A part of something.
184.	Peak: Peek: Pique:	The top of something. (The "a" resembles a mountain top.) To take a quick look. (The two "Es" are for "eyes.") A bit of annoyance or anger. Interest/attract.
185.	Peal Peel:	To ring out. To remove the exterior of something. Skin, rind, or covering.
186.	Pedal: Peddle: Petal:	A foot handle that is used to move a bike forward. To sell. To advertise or publicize. Part of a flower that radiates from the center.
187.	Peer: Pier:	To look at. (The two "Es" are for "eyes.") A walkway that extends from the shore into a body of water.
188.	Pi: Pie:	A geometric measurement, roughly 22/7. A sweet dessert baked on a crust in a circular pan.
189.	Picture: Pitcher:	An image taken with a camera. A large vessel into which several cups of beverage are placed & stored.
190.	Plain: Plane:	Something simple, without adornment. Clear/evident. An aircraft; a geometric concept of two dimensions.
191.	Pleas: Please:	Requests. Short for "if you please." To make someone happy.

192.	Plum:	A small, round purple fruit.
	Plumb:	A weight attached to a line. Exactly or completely.
193.	Pole:	A long thin, round stick.
	Poll:	A place to vote.
194.	Poor:	Not having much money. Pitiful.
	Pore:	A hole or minute opening.
	Pour:	Cause to flow; rain heavily.
195.	Praise:	To compliment.
	Prays:	To request something, typically used in a religious sense.
	Preys:	To stalk.
196.	Principal:	The person who runs a school.
	Principle:	An important or guiding point.
197.	Presence:	The physical existence of someone and something in a particular place.
	Presents:	Gifts.
198.	Pros:	Short form of the word professionals.
	Prose:	Non-poetic writing.
199.	Quiet:	To calm or to silence.
	Quite:	Enough.
		Near homonym.
200.	Rack:	A framework for holding goods.
	Wrack:	Something that is ruined.
201.	Racket:	Noise or clamor. Illegal enterprise.
	Racquet:	Tool used in tennis and badminton.
202.	Rain:	Water that falls from the sky. To pour or shower.
	Reign:	To rule. Time in office/power. (Match the "g" with "regal" or "government.")
	Rein:	Bridle, harness, or strap. (Match the "in" with a strap that can be measured in *in*ches.)
203.	Raise:	To lift up, increase, or improve.
	Rays:	Geometry: straight lines that emanate from a point. Beams of light from the sun.
	Raze:	To cut down to ground level, demolish, annihilate.
204.	Rap:	A sharp knock. A form of music.
	Wrap:	To cover with something.
205.	Read:	To decode letters and derive meaning, past tense.
	Red:	A bright color.
206.	Read:	To decode letters and derive meaning.
	Reed:	A tall, slender grass plant.

207.	Real:	True.
	Reel:	A spool on which things are wound.
208.	Reck:	An old term for worry or care.
	Wreck:	A ruined hulk.
209.	Reek:	To stink.
	Wreak:	To avenge.
210.	Residence:	A house.
	Residents:	People who live in a home or community.
211.	Review:	To look over.
	Revue:	A theatrical production made up of short skits.
212.	Rigger:	One who rigs (or prepares things for use).
	Rigor:	High degree of difficulty, high expectations. Fever or chills.
	Rigueur:	Part of the term "de rigueur" and means required by custom or fashion.
213.	Right:	Correct; opposite of left.
	Rite:	A ritual.
	-Wright:	A craftsman, such as a playwright or wheelwright.
	Write:	To put pen to paper.
214.	Ring:	A band or circle. A piece of jewelry worn on a finger.
	Wring:	To twist something.
215.	Road:	A path.
	Rode:	Form of ride, past tense.
	Rowed:	Move a boat through water using an oar, past tense.
216.	Roe:	Fish eggs.
	Row:	To put oars in the water and pull in order to propel a boat.
217.	Roil:	To stir up.
	Royal:	Someone/thing related to the ruling family of a country.
218.	Role:	A job description. A set of expected behaviors.
	Roll:	A list; in school, the students in a class.
219.	Root:	The bottom of a plant. The basic or bottom part of something.
	Route:	A path.
220.	Rote:	Memory.
	Wrote:	To put pen to paper, past tense.
221.	Rough:	Not smooth.
	Ruff:	A fancy pleated collar. Neck hair or feathers.
222.	Rout:	Tumult, disorder, riot. To thoroughly defeat; to trounce.
	Route:	A path.

223.	Rung: Wrung:	A step on a ladder. To sound a bell, past tense. To squeeze liquid from cloth by twisting it, past tense.
224.	Sail: Sale:	To glide smoothly across something, typically water. A canvas cloth used on a sailboat. An event in which prices are marked down.
225.	Sawed: Sod:	To saw, past tense. Grass with matted roots.
226.	Scene: Seen:	Setting, location. To see, participle.
227.	Sea: See:	A good-sized body of water that is smaller than an ocean. To use the eyes to observe things.
228.	Sear: Seer:	To quickly burn the exterior. A prophet; one who sees. (Match the two "Es" with "eyes.")
229.	Seam: Seem:	The place where two pieces of fabric are sewn together. Appears.
230.	Seas: Sees: Seize:	Bodies of water larger than lakes and smaller than oceans. To use the eyes to observe things. To grab something.
231.	Serge: Surge:	To bind the edges of fabric (as with a serger). To move ahead quickly.
232.	Sew: So: Sow:	Use needle and thread to join two pieces of fabric. A coordinating conjunction used to join two simple sentences. A subordinating conjunction meaning *in order to*. To plant seeds.
233.	Shear: Sheer:	To cut off, shave, clip, or trim. Adjective meaning pure/complete or steep/vertical.
234.	Shone: Shown:	To shine, past tense. To show or display, participle.
235.	Sighs: Size:	Breaths that are long and loud. How much something measures.
236.	Slew: Slough:	To slay (or kill), past tense. Deep muddy area; swamp.
237.	Sloe: Slow:	Small, round, dark fruit of the blackthorn. To move at an unhurried pace.
238.	Soar: Sore:	To fly high. A painful place. To be in pain.
239.	Sole: Soul:	Only. A type of fish. Bottom of the foot. The internal part of a person, not related to the body.

240.	Some: Sum:	Part of something or a group. Total.
241.	Son: Sun:	Male offspring. A star around which planets rotate.
242.	Sot: Sought:	A drunk or alcoholic. To look for, past tense.
243.	Sough: Sue:	When the wind makes a sighing or moaning sound. To take someone to court for payment of a debt or to right a wrong.
244.	Staff: Staph:	Employees. Short term for staphylococcus, which causes serious infections.
245.	Stair: Stare:	A step(s) leading from one level to another. To look at for a long period of time, typically without blinking.
246.	Stalk: Stock:	To quietly follow with the intention of doing harm. Products on hand.
247.	Steal: Steel:	To take without permission. Very strong metal.
248.	Stile: Style:	Steps for climbing over a fence. Fashion or method.
249.	Straight: Strait:	In a direct line. A narrow body of water, often between cliffs.
250.	Suite: Sweat: Sweet:	A set of rooms or matching furniture. A set of instrumental works played together. Perspiration. *Near homonym.* Pleasant. Tasty or kind.
251.	Tacks: Tax:	Small nails with broad heads and short metal spikes. When the government requires a portion of a person's income as a way of financing its (the government's) expenses.
252.	Tail: Tale:	The end of something. A story.
253.	Tare: Tear:	An old word for a weed. To rip or slash. A slit or split.
254.	Tea: Tee:	A hot drink brewed from tasty leaves. The small wooden peg that holds a golf ball for a player.
255.	Team: Teem:	A group or band. A side or players. To swarm or abound.

256.	Tear:	A drop of moisture when one cries.
	Tier:	A row, level, or layer.
257.	Their:	Possessive pronoun meaning that several people own something.
	There:	Not here.
	They're	Contraction of the words *they* and *are*.
258.	Threw:	To throw. (Match the "e" with elbow.)
	Through:	Preposition meaning to pass between.
259.	Thyme:	A seasoning.
	Time:	Minute or hour. System of distinguishing events.
260.	Tide:	The ebb and flow of salt water.
	Tied:	To join with a knot, past tense.
261.	To:	A preposition.
	Too:	Adverb meaning extra or also.
	Two:	More than one, less than three.
262.	Toe:	One of the digits on a human foot.
	Tow:	To pull behind.
263.	Trader:	One who trades.
	Traitor:	One who has betrayed others.
264.	Vain:	Conceited or proud. Ineffective or hopeless.
	Vane:	A rotating blade.
	Vein:	A blood vessel that returns blood to the heart.
265.	Vary:	Differ.
	Very:	An adverb showing emphasis.
266.	Verses:	Groups of lines in a song or poem.
	Versus:	Against.
267.	Wade:	To walk in shallow water.
	Weighed:	To check on one's weight, past tense.
268.	Wail:	To cry aloud.
	Wale:	A ridge of fabric. A skin welt.
	Whale:	A large, sea-dwelling mammal.
269.	Waist:	The place about the middle of an object; it can be measured in inches (match it up with the "i" for inches).
	Waste:	Trash (match it up with the "e" for environment).
270.	Wait:	To pause.
	Weight:	Heaviness, mass, burden. Can also mean influence or emphasis.
271.	Waive:	To give up something voluntarily.
	Wave:	Move the hand repeatedly as a signal. Moving ripple on the ocean.

272.	Walk:	To move forward at a measured pace.
	Wok:	A Chinese cooking pan.
273.	Wan:	Pale.
	Won:	To achieve a victory, past tense.
274.	War:	A conflict.
	Wore:	To put on (clothes), past tense.
275.	Ware:	Product for sale.
	Wear:	To put on.
	Where:	A place.
276.	Way:	A road or path.
	Weigh:	To determine the size or mass.
277.	We:	A pronoun that includes a group plus oneself.
	Wee:	An old term for small.
	Whee:	An interjection that expresses excitement.
278.	Weak:	Not strong.
	Week:	7 days.
279.	Weather:	Conditions in the atmosphere.
	Whether:	If.
280	Which:	Choose between two possibilities.
	Witch:	Member of the Wiccan faith.
281.	While:	During.
	Wile:	Cunning intelligence. To lazily pass time.
282.	Whine:	To moan in a high pitched voice.
	Wine:	An alcoholic beverage typically made from grapes or berries.
283.	Whirled:	To spin, past tense.
	World:	A planet.
284.	Woman:	One female human.
	Women:	Two or more females.
		Near homonyms; often confused.
285.	Wood:	The trunk of a tree.
	Would:	Helping verb indicating that something can be done.
286.	Yawn:	A wide opening of the mouth that occurs when one is sleepy.
	Yon:	Old term for "over there."
287.	Yoke:	Wooden harness used to group animals to work together.
	Yolk:	The yellow part of an egg.

288.	Yore:	The old days.
	You're:	Contraction of the words *you* and *are*.
	Your:	Possessive pronoun meaning that you own something.
289.	You'll:	Contraction for *you* and *will*.
	Yule:	Related to Christmas.

PUZZLE KEYS

Homonyms 1-10, Puzzle 1

ACROSS: 4-hale, 5-cash, 8-faint, 9-cache, 10-idle,
11-idol, 12-alot, 14-gait, 15-knead, 17-need. DOWN:
1-ewe, 2-dawn, 3-gate, 6-hail, 7-bail, 8-feint, 12-allot,
13-bale, 15-knead, 16-don.

Puzzle 2

1-cash, 2-ewe, 3-hale, 4-allot, 5-gait, 6-feint,
7-kneed, 8-don, 9-alot, 10-cache, 11-dawn,
12-you, 13-need, 14-faint, 15-gate, 16- hail,
17-idol, 18-knead, 19-idle, 20-bale, 21-bail.

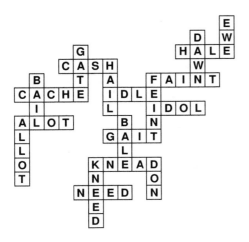

Puzzle 3

ACROSS: 4-hale, 6-alot, 7-feint, 13-don, 14-allot,
15-gate, 16-bail, 18-cache, 19-kneed. DOWN: 1-cash
2-gait, 3-you, 5-ewe, 7-faint, 8-need, 9-idol, 10-knead
11-idle, 12-hail, 16-bale, 17-dawn.

Puzzle 4

1-idle, 2-cash, 3-ewe, 4-idol, 5-hale, 6-feint,
7-kneed, 8-gate, 9-don, 10-alot, 11-cache,
12-dawn, 13-allot, 14-gait, 15-need, 16-faint,
17-hail, 18-knead, 19-you, 20-bale, 21-bail.

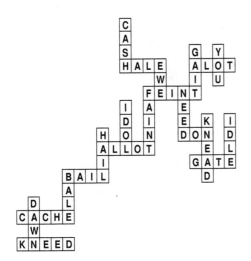

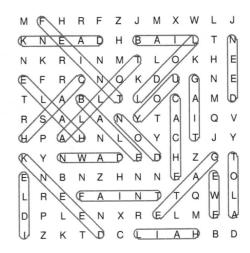

Homonyms 11-20, Puzzle 1

ACROSS: 2-wrack, 3-quiet, 6-tax, 8-rack, 9-vane, 12-vain, 13-paced, 14-sail, 15-made, 16-ore, 17-lain, 18-or. DOWN: 1-paste, 3-quite, 4-tacks, 5-naval, 7-lane, 10-navel, 11-sale, 12-vein, 15-maid, 16-oar.

Puzzle 2

1-paste, 2-quite, 3-navel, 4-wrack, 5-lain, 6-vane, 7-made, 8-naval, 9-oar, 10-sale, 11-ore, 12-lane, 13-paced, 14-quiet, 15-rack, 16-sail, 17-maid, 18-tacks, 19-vain, 20-or, 21-vein, 22-tax.

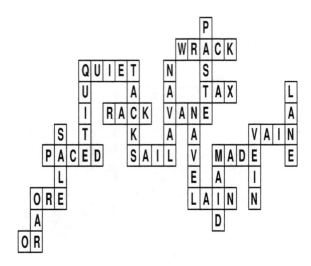

Puzzle 3

ACROSS: 1-mode, 3-vain, 5-quiet, 9-navel, 10-or, 11-tax, 12-wrack, 13-lane, 14-sale, 16-vane, 17-paste. DOWN: 1-maid, 2-sail, 4-naval, 5-quite, 6-tacks, 7-rack, 8-oar, 10-ore, 15-lain, 16-vein, 17-paced.

Puzzle 4

1-paste, 2-quite, 3-lane, 4-navel, 5-vane, 6-wrack, 7-made, 8-naval, 9-oar, 10-lain, 11-ore, 12-paced, 13-tacks, 14-rack, 15-sail, 16-maid, 17-vain, 18-sale, 19-quiet, 20-or, 21-vein, 22-tax.

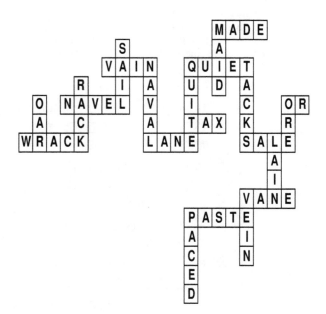

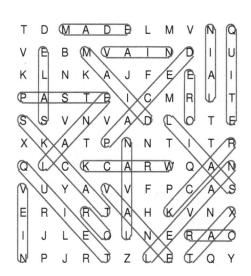

Homonyms 21-30, Puzzle 1

ACROSS: 2-fair, 6-new, 9-fare, 10-bait, 11-hair, 12-except, 15-yon, 16-wade, 17-days, 19-gnu, 20-in, 21-knew. DOWN: 1-hare, 2-faire, 3-inn, 4-bate, 5-daze, 7-weighed, 8-callous, 13-callus, 14-yawn, 18-accept.

Puzzle 2

1-wade, 2-gnu, 3-daze, 4-hare, 5-yawn, 6-days, 7-bait, 8-fare, 9-bate, 10-callus, 11-accept, 12-yon, 13-weighed, 14-faire, 15-knew, 16-hair, 17-in, 18-fair, 19-new, 20-inn, 21-except, 22-callous.

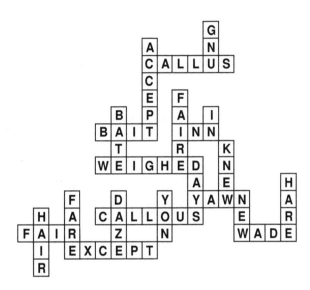

Puzzle 3

ACROSS: 2-fair, 4-days, 7-hair, 10-new, 12-bate, 13-except, 14-gnu, 17, bait, 18-fare, 19-knew, 20-inn. DOWN: 1-callus, 3-faire, 4-daze, 5-yon, 6-callous, 8-accept, 9-wade, 11-weighed, 15-hare, 16-yawn, 20-in.

Puzzle 4

1-wade, 2-gnu, 3-faire, 4-daze, 5-hare, 6-days, 7-bait, 8-fare, 9-bate, 10-callus, 11-accept, 12-yon, 13-knew, 14-hair, 15-callous, 16-in, 17-yawn, 18-fair, 19-new, 20-inn, 21-except, 22-weighed.

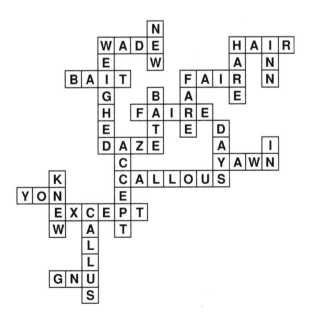

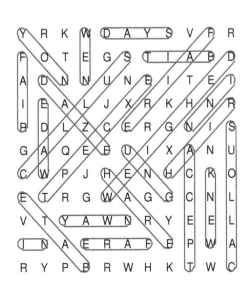

202

Homonyms 31-40, Puzzle 1

ACROSS: 1-sod, 2-layer, 6-won, 8-racket, 10-vary,
11-none, 12-night, 13-male, 14-pale, 15-tale. DOWN:
1-sawed, 2-lair, 3-racquet, 4-one, 5-knight, 7-nun,
9-tail, 10-very, 13-mail, 14-pail.

Puzzle 2

1-pale, 2-tale, 3-knight, 4-one, 5-male, 6-tail,
7-pail, 8-sawed, 9-very, 10-night, 11-racquet,
12-lair, 13-won, 14-mail, 15-vary, 16-vary,
17-none, 18-sod, 19-layer, 20-nun.

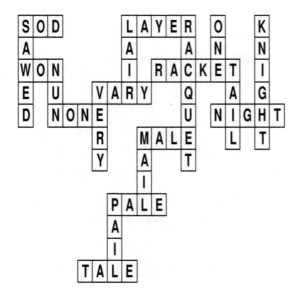

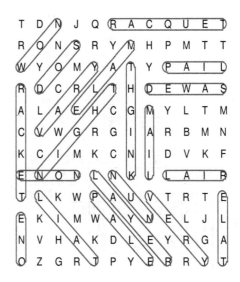

Puzzle 3

ACROSS: 3-mail, 7-pale, 8-tail, 9-racquet, 11-very,
12-none, 14-layer, 15-night, 16-won, 17-sod. DOWN:
1-pail, 2-one, 4-lain, 5-male, 6-racket, 8-tale, 10-knight,
11-vary, 13-sawed, 15-nun.

Puzzle 4

1-tale, 2-racket, 3-knight, 4-ore, 5-vary, 6-male,
7-pale, 8-tail, 9-sawed, 10-very, 11-night,
12-racquet, 13-layer, 14-lair, 15-pail, 16-won,
17-mail, 18-none, 19-sod, 20-nun.

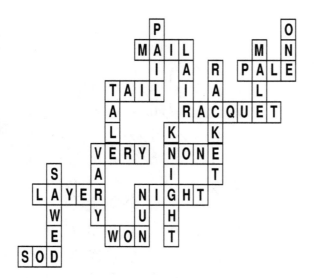

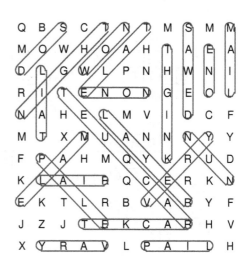

Homonyms 41-50, Puzzle 1
ACROSS: 4-deer, 5-yolk, 7-wale, 9-bawl, 13-dear,
15-instants, 17-whale, 18-ball, 19-have, 21- instance,
22-fairy. DOWN: 1-gorilla, 2-half, 3-ferry, 5-yoke,
6-can't, 8-adds, 10-wail, 11-halve, 12-guerilla, 14-cant,
16-ads, 20-adz.

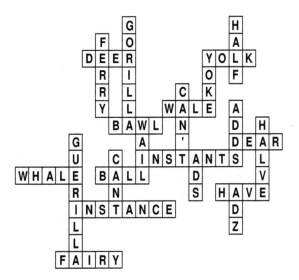

Puzzle 2
1-wail, 2-ads, 3-yolk, 4-adds, 5-deer, 6-ball,
7-gorilla, 8-bawl, 9-wale, 10-can't, 11-dear,
12-fairy, 13-whale, 14-half, 15-ferry, 16-cant,
17-guerilla, 17-halve, 19-adz, 20-have,
21-instance, 22-yoke, 23-instants.

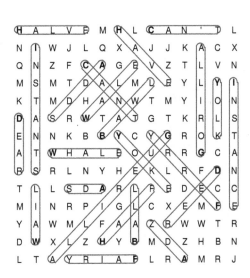

Puzzle 3
ACROSS: 3-half, 5-can't, 6-have, 8-instants, 10-yoke
12-deer, 14-adds, 16-ferry, 17-adz, 18-wale, 19-bawl,
20-ball. DOWN: 1-yolk, 2-whale, 4-fairy, 5-cant,
7-guerilla, 8-instance, 9-halve, 11-ads, 13-gorilla,
15-dear, 18-wail.

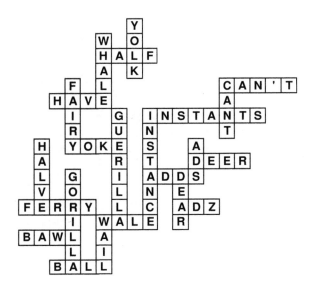

Puzzle 4
1-wail, 2-instance, 3-ads, 4-adds, 5-deer, 6-ball,
7-dear, 8-gorilla, 9-bawl, 10-wale, 11-ferry,
12-can't, 13-fairy, 14-whale, 15-have, 16-half,
17-guerilla, 18-yolk, 19-halve, 20-cant, 21-adz,
22-yoke, 23-instants.

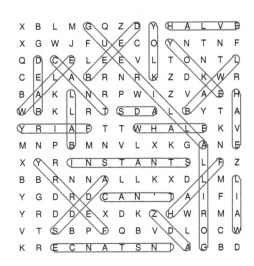

Homonyms 51-60, Puzzle 1

ACROSS: 3-seen, 4-not, 6-knot, 10-tare, 12-waist, 14-lay, 15-Maine, 16-verses, 20-lei, 21-scene, 22-naught.
DOWN: 1-main, 2-rein, 5-ordinance, 7-ordnance, 8-versus, 9-reign, 11-pane, 13-pain, 15-mane, 17-rain, 18-waste, 19-fear.

Puzzle 2

1-waste, 2-knot, 3-pain, 4-not, 5-lay, 6-versus, 7-tare, 8-main, 9-Maine, 10-ordinance, 11-ordnance, 12-pane, 13-rain, 14-naught, 15-rein, 16-seems, 17-seen, 18-tear, 19-verses, 20-reign, 21-waist, 22-mane, 23-lei.

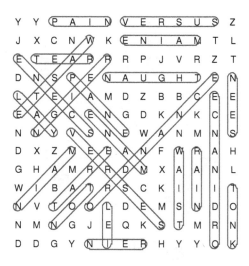

Puzzle 3

ACROSS: 4-pain, 8-ordnance, 9-reign, 10-lei, 11-pane, 12-versus, 19-tare, 20-ordinance, 21-scene, 22-naught.
DOWN: 1-waste, 2-knot, 3-rain, 5-mane, 6-verses, 7-main, 10-lay, 13-rain, 14-Maine, 15-waist, 16-tear, 17-not, 18-seen.

Puzzle 4

1-waste, 2-ordnance, 3-knot, 4-pain, 5-versus, 6-tare, 7-main, 8-Maine, 9-ordnance, 10-waist, 11-pane, 12-naught, 13-rein, 14-not, 15-reign, 16-scene, 17-seen, 18-tear, 19-lay, 20-verses, 21-mane, 22-rain, 23-lei.

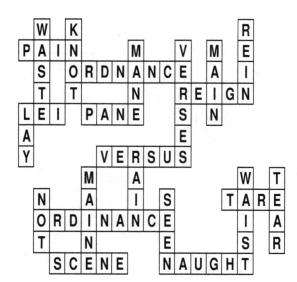

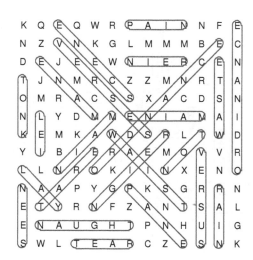

Homonyms 61-70, Puzzle 1

ACROSS: 1-hearty, 3-great, 4-yore, 7-grate, 10-aid, 11-its, 12-banned, 15-faun, 16-know, 17-canvas, 18-no,
DOWN: 1-hardy, 2-you're, 4-your, 5-den, 6-band, 8-aide, 9-canvass, 11-it's, 13-ade, 14-din, 15-fawn.

Puzzle 2

1-yore, 2-canvas, 3-aid, 4-you're, 5-great, 6-your, 7-ade, 8-no, 9-banned, 10-it's, 11-aide, 12-canvass, 13-den, 14-hardy, 15-din, 16-fawn, 17-know, 18-grate, 19-band, 20-hearty, 21-its, 22-fawn.

Puzzle 3

ACROSS: 1-faun, 3-ade, 8-grate, 9-your, 10-canvas, 11-no, 12-band, 13-fawn, 14-you're, 16-its, 17-den.
DOWN: 2-aid, 3-aide, 4-it's, 5-hardy, 6-great, 7-know, 9-yore, 10-canvass, 12-banned, 15-din.

Puzzle 4

1-aid, 2-yore, 3-canvas, 4-great, 5-your, 6-ade, 7-faun, 8-no, 9-it's, 10-aide, 11-canvass, 12-den, 13-you're, 14-hardy, 15-fawn, 16-din, 17-know, 18-grate, 19-banned, 20-band, 21-hearty, 22-its.

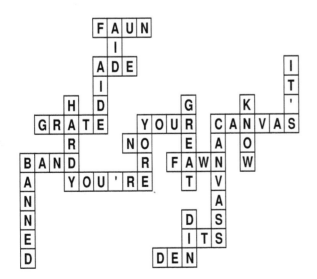

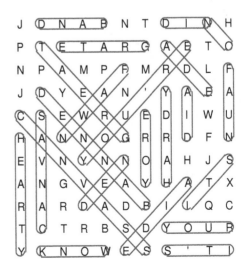

Homonyms 71-80, Puzzle 1

ACROSS: 1-wait, 4-lays, 5-rays, 7-see, 9-maize, 10-bare, 11-pear, 13-you'll, 15-laze, 16-effect, 18-weight, 19-bear, DOWN: 2-tea, 3-raise, 5-raze, 6-sea, 8-pair, 11-pare, 12-affect, 13-yule, 14-maze, 17-tea.

Puzzle 2

1-wait, 2-lays, 3-maize, 4-pare, 5-bare, 6-tea, 7-pear, 8-raise, 9-rays, 10-raze, 11-sea, 12- effect, 13-maze, 14-see, 15-laze, 16-tea, 17-weight, 18-you'll, 19-pair, 20-yule, 21-affect, 22-bear.

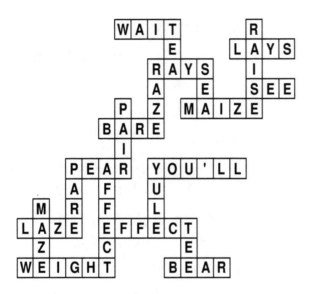

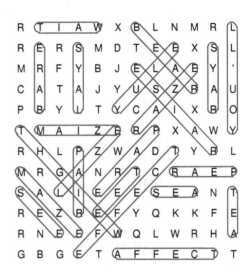

Puzzle 3

ACROSS: 2-weight, 4-pare, 5-sea, 8-pear, 9-bare, 10-rays, 13-maze, 15-wait, 16-bear, 18-lays, 19-effect, 20-tea. DOWN: 1-yule, 3-tea, 4-pair, 5-see, 6-laze, 7-maize, 11-you'll, 12-raise, 14-affect, 17-raze.

Puzzle 4

1-lays, 2-maize, 3-pare, 4-bare, 5-wait, 6-yule, 7-raze, 8-pear, 9-raise, 10-rays, 11-sea, 12-laze, 13-effect, 14-maze, 15-tea, 16-see, 17-affect, 18-tea, 19-weight, 20-you'll, 21-pair, 22-bear.

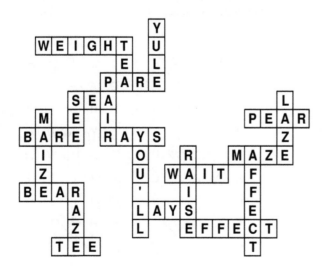

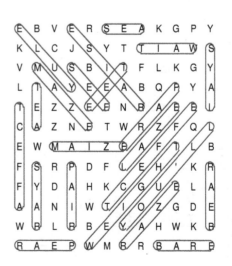

Homonyms 81-90, Puzzle 1

ACROSS: 3-mall, 6-fond, 8-heart, 10-desert, 11-leach, 13-past, 14-wrap, 16-grown, 17-groan, 18-passed.
DOWN: 1-maul, 2-capital, 4-knows, 5-leach, 7-nose, 8-hart, 9-rap, 10-dessert, 12-capitol, 15-fawned.

Puzzle 2

1-capital, 2-groan, 3-leech, 4-capitol, 5-hart, 6-desert, 7-maul, 8-dessert, 9-fond, 10-wrap, 11-grown, 12-heart, 13-known, 14-leach, 15-mall, 16-passed, 17-fawned, 18-past, 19-nose, 20-rap.

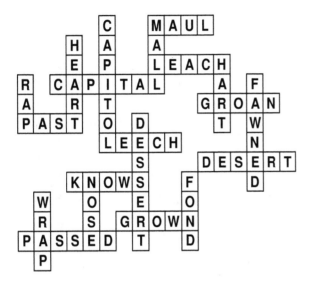

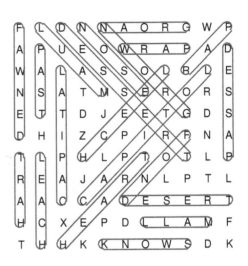

Puzzle 3

ACROSS: 4-fawned, 8-wrap, 9-passed, 10-rap, 11-leach, 13-past, 14-capital, 17-hart, 18-nose, 19-capitol. DOWN: 1-knows, 2-grown, 3-groad, 4-fond, 5-desert, 6-dessert, 7-maul, 12-heart, 15-leach, 16-mall.

Puzzle 4

1-groan, 2-leech, 3-wrap, 4-capitol, 5-maul, 6-passed, 7-hart, 8-capital, 9-fond, 10-grown, 11-heart, 11-knows, 13-leach, 14-mall, 15-dessert, 16-fawned, 17-desert, 18-past, 19-nose, 20-rap.

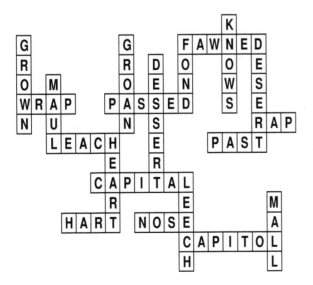

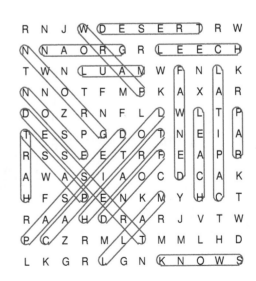

Homonyms 91-100, Puzzle 1

ACROSS: 1-seer, 5-ail, 6-karat, 7-guest, 9-feat, 11-ale, 12-due, 13-waive, 14-teem, 15-do. DOWN: 1-sear, 2-carat, 3-barre, 4-wave, 7-guessed, 8-carrot, 9-feet, 10-team, 12-dew.

Puzzle 2

1-sear, 2-feat, 3-karat, 4-carrot, 5-ail, 6-team, 7-teem, 8-bar, 9-waive, 10-hat, 11-wave, 12-ale, 13-guest, 14-feet, 15-barre, 16-carat, 17-dew, 18-do, 19-due, 20-seer, 21-guessed, 22-hay.

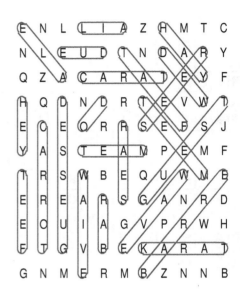

Puzzle 3

ACROSS: 3-carat, 4-do, 9-ail, 10-wave, 11-guessed, 13-barre 14-feat, 16-carrot, 17-team. DOWN: 1-feat, 2-waive, 4-dew, 5-karat, 6-ale, 7-sear, 8-teem, 11-guest, 12-due, 13-bar, 15-hay.

Puzzle 4

1-feat, 2-guest, 3-karat, 4-carrot, 5-ail, 6-feet, 7-team, 8-teem, 9-waive, 10-hay, 11-sear, 12-wave, 13-ale, 14-carat, 15-dew, 16-bar, 17-do, 18-due, 19-seer, 20-guessed, 21-barre, 22-hey.

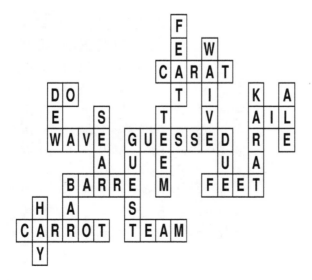

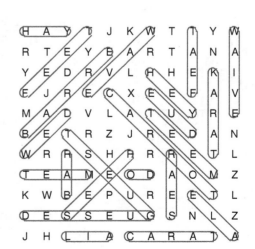

Homonyms 101-110, Puzzle 1

ACROSS: 2-tear, 3-seem, 6-patience, 8-castor, 10-heir, 11-basis, 12-air, 13-seam, 15-leak, 16-walk, 17-leak.
DOWN: 1-patients, 4-mantle, 5-red, 7-tier, 8-caster, 9-read, 11-bases, 14-mantel, 16-wok.

Puzzle 2

1-red, 2-leak, 3-seem, 4-heir, 5-mantle, 6-patients, 7-read, 8-basis, 9-wok, 10-seam, 11-tear, 12-mantel, 13-tier, 14-leek, 15-walk, 16-caster, 17-air, 18-bases, 19-patients, 20-castor.

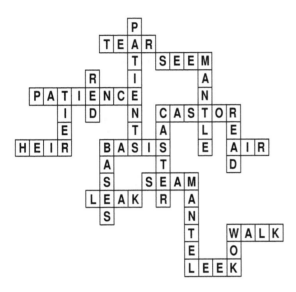

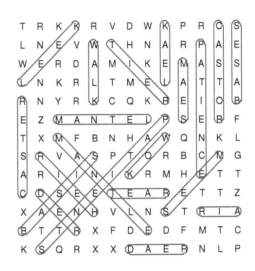

Puzzle 3

ACROSS: 3-leak, 5-patients, 7-caster, 11-air, 12-tear 14-patients, 16-wok, 17-mantel, 18-seem. DOWN: 1-walk, 2-tier, 3-leek, 4-mantle, 6-heir, 7-castor, 8-basis, 9-bases, 10-seam, 13-read, 15-red.

Puzzle 4

1-red, 2-mantle, 3-air, 4-leak, 5-seem, 6-heir, 7-basis, 8-patients, 9-read, 10-tier, 11-wok, 12-tear, 13-mantel, 14-patients, 15-leek, 16-walk, 17-caster, 18-bases, 19-castor, 20-seam.

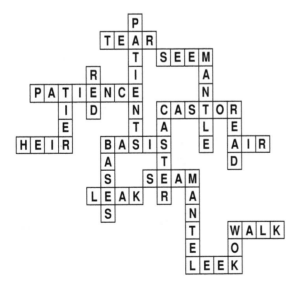

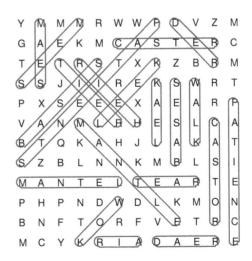

Homonyms 111-120, Puzzle 1

ACROSS: 3-seas, 4-they're, 5-there, 6-paws, 7-lien, 8-read, 9-mayor, 11-heel, 13-fined, 15-won, 16-lean, DOWN: 1-sees, 2-heal, 3-seize, 5-their, 6-pause, 8-reed, 9-mane, 10-find, 12-die, 14-dye, 15-wan.

Puzzle 2

1-find, 2-reed, 3-seize, 4-die, 5-there, 6-paws, 7-wan, 8-fined, 9-heal, 10-sees, 11-mare, 12-they're, 13-heel, 14-lien, 15-mayor, 16-pause, 17-lean, 18-read, 19-dye, 20-seas, 21-their, 22-won.

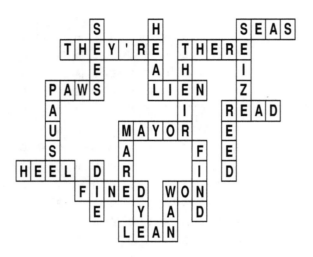

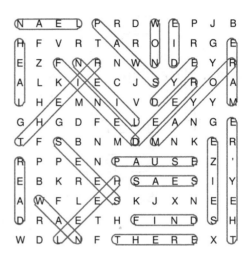

Puzzle 3

ACROSS: 1-won, 3-reed, 5-find, 6-read, 8-lean, 9-there, 12-they're, 13-dye, 14-pause, 17-mayor, 18-heel, 19-seas. DOWN: 1-wan, 2-mare, 4-die, 5-fined, 7-their, 8-lien, 10-heal, 11-seize, 15-sees, 16-paws.

Puzzle 4

1-wan, 2-there, 3-find, 4-dye, 5-fined, 6-reed, 7-seize, 8-die, 9-paws, 10-mayor, 11-heal, 12-won, 13-sees, 14-mare, 15-they're, 16-heel, 17-lien, 18-pause, 19-lean, 20-read, 21-seas, 22-their.

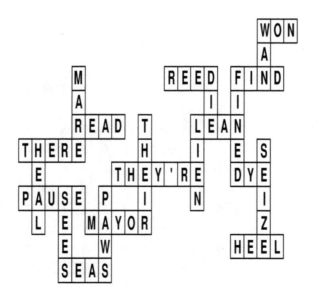

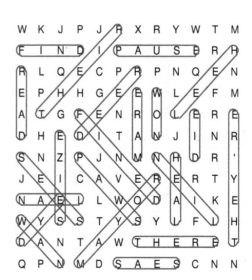

Homonyms 121-130, Puzzle 1

ACROSS: 1-Bea, 3-led, 6-pea, 8-real, 10-died, 11-aisle 12-I'll, 13-marry, 14-be, 15-here, 16-caught. DOWN: 1-bee, 2-flare, 3-lead, 4-dyed, 5-flair, 6-pee, 7-reel, 8-Mary, 12-isle, 13-merry, 15-hear.

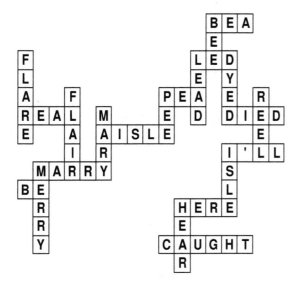

Puzzle 2

1-be, 2-I'll, 3-bee, 4-caught, 5-here, 6-cot, 7-dyed, 8-isle, 9-flair, 10-real, 11-flare, 12-hear, 13-led, 14-pea, 15-Mary, 16-died, 17-lead, 18-marry, 19-Bea, 20-aisle, 21-merry, 22-pee, 23-reel.

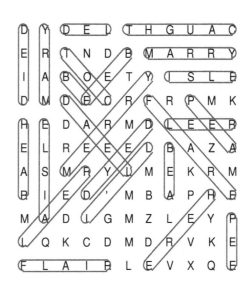

Puzzle 3

ACROSS: 3-hear, 5-caught, 7-flare, 8-Bea, 9-pea, 11-I'll, 13-marry, 15-isle, 16-marry, 17-dyed, 18-led, 19-bee. DOWN: 1-reel, 2-cot, 4-be, 6-here, 7-flair, 8-pee, 10-aisle, 12-lead, 13-Mary, 14-real, 17-died.

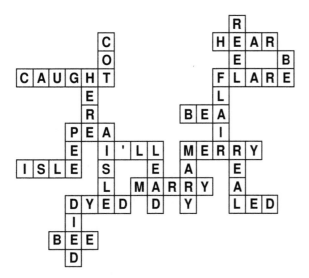

Puzzle 4

1-I'll, 2-real, 3-bee, 4-Mary, 5-caught, 6-here, 7-merry, 8-cot, 9-dyed, 10-isle, 11-hear, 12-Bea, 13-led, 14-be, 15-pea, 16-died, 17-flair, 18-lead, 19-marry, 20-flare, 21-aisle, 22-pee, 23-reel.

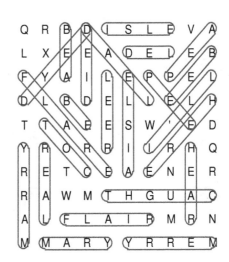

212

Homonyms 131-140, Puzzle 1

ACROSS: 1-flee, 3-beech, 6-sew, 7-all, 8-war, 10-through, 11-dough, 14-so, 15-cawed, 17-herd, 18-Lent. DOWN: 1-flea, 2-beach, 4-heard, 5-awl, 8-sow, 10-threw, 12-ware, 13-lint, 15-cod, 16-doe.

Puzzle 2

1-sew, 2-so, 3-dough, 4-threw, 5-cod, 6-war, 7-beech, 8-flea, 9-all, 10-beach, 11-sow, 12-cawed, 13-doe, 14-Lent, 15-flee, 16-heard, 17-awl, 18-wore, 19-herd, 20-through, 21-lint.

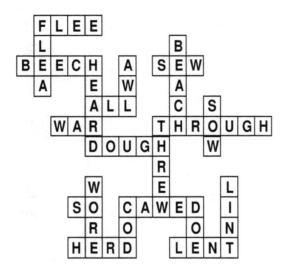

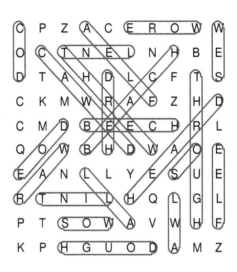

Puzzle 3

ACROSS: 3-dough, 5-beach, 7-flee, 8-war, 10-wore, 12-all, 14-Lent, 15-heard, 17-cod, 18-through. DOWN: 1-so, 2-threw, 4-sew, 6-cawed, 7-flea, 9-awl, 11-beech, 13-lint, 15-sow, 16-doe, 20-herd.

Puzzle 4

1-so, 2-all, 3-dough, 4-threw, 5-war, 6-beech, 7-flea, 8-wore, 9-beach, 10-sow, 11-cawed, 12-doe, 13-through, 14-Lent, 15-sew, 16-flee, 17-heard, 18-awl, 19-herd, 20-cod, 21-lint.

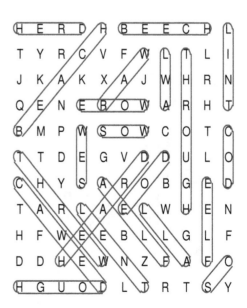

Homonyms 141-150, Puzzle 1

ACROSS: 2-thyme, 5-wreck, 8-allowed, 9-shear,
10-wear, 12-time, 14-peace, 15-does, 16-ware, 17-beat.
DOWN: 1-sheer, 3-meat, 4-aloud, 5-where, 6-cede,
7-beet, 9-seed, 11-reck, 13-meet, 14-piece, 15-dose.

Puzzle 2

1-peace, 2-meet, 3-where, 4-piece, 5-wreck,
6-beat, 7-cede, 8-meat, 9-shear, 10-does,
11-thyme, 12-ware, 13-allowed, 14-reck,
15-aloud, 16-beet, 17-time, 18-seed, 19-sheer,
20-wear, 21-dose.

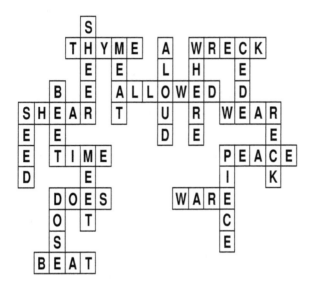

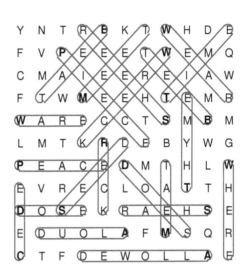

Puzzle 3

ACROSS: 1-beet, 4-meet, 5-meat, 8-seed, 10-shear,
13-ware, 15-dose, 16-cede, 17-does, 18-wreck,
19-allowed. DOWN: 1-beat, 2-thyme, 3-where, 6-time,
7-wear, 9-peace, 10-sheer, 11-aloud, 12-reck, 14-piece.

Puzzle 4

1-shear, 2-meet, 3-where, 4-aloud, 5-piece,
6-wreck, 7-thyme, 8-cede, 9-meat, 10-seed,
11-does, 12-ware, 13-allowed, 14-beat, 15-wear,
16-reck, 17-beet, 18-time, 19-peace, 20-sheer,
21-dose.

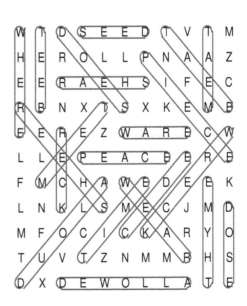

Homonyms 151-160, Puzzle 1

ACROSS: 2-shown, 3-weigh, 5-lintel, 8-metal, 9-eight, 11-flees, 13-tied, 15-wreak, 16-medal, 17-ate, 18-peek.
DOWN: 1-reek, 2-shone, 4-fleece, 5-lintel, 6-high, 7-meddle, 10-hi, 11-fleas, 12-pique, 13-tide, 14-peak, 15-way.

Puzzle 2

1-flees, 2-hi, 3-lentil, 4-reek, 5-pique, 6-medal, 7-tide, 8-fleas, 9-shone, 10-metal, 11-way, 12-peak, 13-high, 14-peek, 15-lintel, 16-wreak, 17-ate, 18-shown, 19-tied, 20-weigh, 21-eight, 22-meddle, 23-fleece.

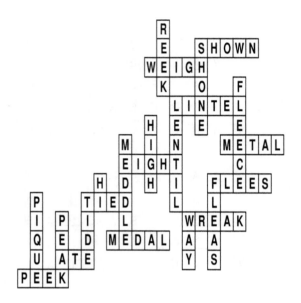

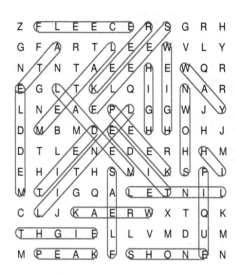

Puzzle 3

ACROSS: 4-pique, 6-weigh, 7-fleas, 8-wreak, 11-lentil, 13-peak, 14-meddle, 15-eight, 17-tied, 18-shone, 19-flees.
DOWN: 1-hi, 2-metal, 3-ate, 5-shown, 6-way, 7-fleece, 9-reek, 10-tide, 12-lintel, 13-peek, 14-medal, 16-high.

Puzzle 4

1-flees, 2-wreak, 3-hi, 4-way, 5-reek, 6-pique, 7-medal, 8-tide, 9-fleas, 10-shone, 11-lintel, 12-meddle, 13-metal, 14-tied, 15-peak, 16-eight, 17-high, 18-peek, 19-ate, 20-shown, 21-weigh, 22-lintel, 23-fleece.

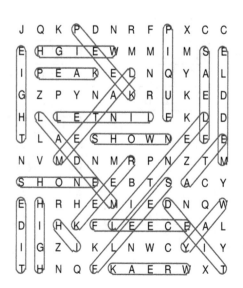

Homonyms 161-170, Puzzle 1

ACROSS: 4-flue, 7-bow, 8-residents, 9-size, 11-doze, 14-mind, 15-peel, 17-hymn, 18-sighs, 19-sealing.
DOWN: 1-lesson, 2-does, 3-flew, 5-lessen, 6-mined, 7-beau, 10-residence, 12-ceiling, 13-flu, 16-peal, 17-him.

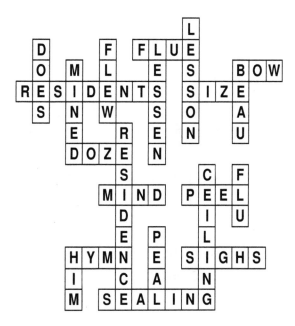

Puzzle 2

1-peal, 2-bow, 3-ceiling, 4-hymn, 5-does, 6-mined, 7-doze, 8-residence, 9-flew, 10-him, 11-sighs, 12-lessen, 13-beau, 14-lesson, 15-sealing, 16-peel, 17-flue, 18-residents, 19-size, 20-flu, 21-mind.

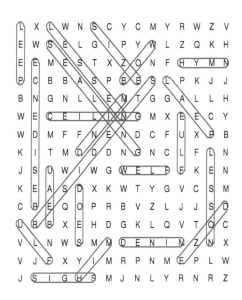

Puzzle 3

ACROSS: 1-hymn, 6-residents, 8-lesson, 10-mined, 12-flew, 13-ceiling, 15-beau, 19-residence, 20-flu.
DOWN: 2-mind, 3-doze, 4-sealing, 5-him, 7-bow, 9-size, 11-does, 12-flue, 14-lessen, 16-peal, 17-sighs, 18-peel.

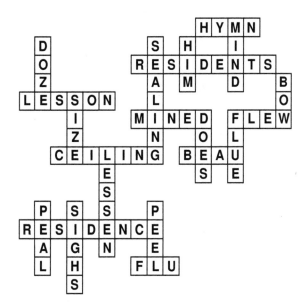

Puzzle 4

1-lessen, 2-residence, 3-peal, 4-bow, 5-ceiling, 6-doze, 7-hymn, 8-peel, 9-does, 10-mined, 11-flew, 12-signs, 13-beau, 14-size, 15-lesson, 16-sealing, 17-him, 18-flue, 19-residents, 20-flu, 21-mind.

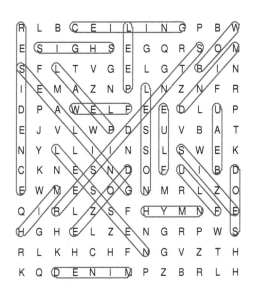

216

Homonyms 171-180, Puzzle 1

ACROSS: 3-Ben, 5-flower, 8-done, 9-we, 10-minor, 14-to, 15-dun, 16-bin, 17-let's, 20-whole, 21-lets.
DOWN: 1-cell, 2-whee, 4-two, 5-flour, 6-wee, 7-been, 10-miner, 11-ought, 12-hole, 13-aught, 18-too, 19-sell.

Puzzle 2

1-aught, 2-to, 3-wee, 4-lets, 5-two, 6-been, 7-flower, 8-whee, 9-ought, 10-Ben, 11-too, 12-sell, 13-miner, 14-bin, 15-dose, 16-dun, 17-flour, 18-whole, 19-let's, 20-minor, 21-cell, 22-hole, 23-we.

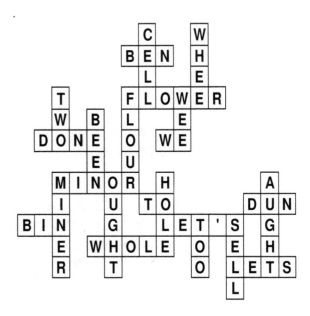

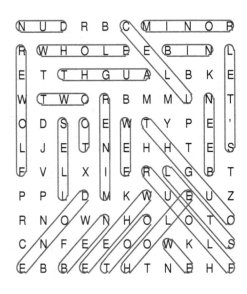

Puzzle 3

ACROSS: 2-two, 4-cell, 5-lets, 8-whee, 9-whole, 10-to, 12-flour, 13-done, 14-Ben, 15-too, 17-we, 18-miner, 19-bin. DOWN: 1-flower, 3-wee, 5-let's, 6-sell, 7-hole, 11-aught, 13-dun, 14-been, 16-ought, 18-minor.

Puzzle 4

1-aught, 2-ought, 3-to, 4-dun, 5-been, 6-wee, 7-lets, 8-two, 9-flower, 10-Ben, 11-whole, 12-too, 13-cell, 14-sell, 15-miner, 16-bin, 17-done, 18-flour, 19-let's, 20-whee, 21-minor, 22-hole, 23-we.

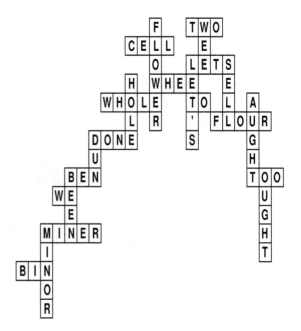

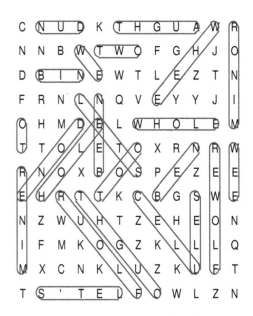

217

Homonyms 181-190, Puzzle 1

ACROSS: 3-away, 5-bear, 6-slough, 8-week, 9-revue, 10-slew, 11-petal, 12-four, 13-toe, 14-review, 15-dual, 16-censor. DOWN: 1-aweigh, 2-duel, 4-fore, 5-bier, 6-sensor, 7-pedal, 8-weak, 11-peddle, 12-for, 13-tow.

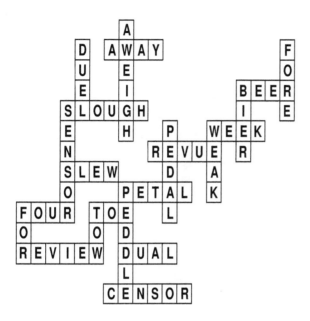

Puzzle 2

1-peddle, 2-week, 3-bier, 4-four, 5-review, 6-slew, 7-dual, 8-tow, 9-weak, 10-sensor, 11-fore, 12-slough, 13-away, 14-pedal, 15-beer, 16-toe, 17-censor, 18-revue, 19-petal, 20-duel, 21-for, 22-aweigh.

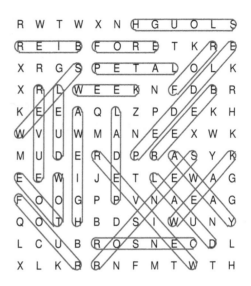

Puzzle 3

ACROSS: 3-toe, 4-revue, 5-away, 7-fore, 9-pedal, 11-sensor, 14-peddle, 15-tow, 16-slough, 17-beer, 18-duel. DOWN: 1-four, 2-petal, 4-review, 6-week, 7-for, 8-weak, 10-aweigh, 12-slew, 13-sensor, 17-bier, 18-dual.

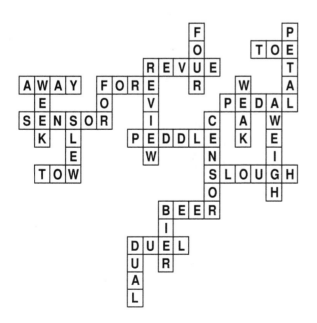

Puzzle 4

1-week, 2-dual, 3-aweigh, 4- bier, 5-four, 6-slew, 7-tow, 8-weak, 9-sensor, 10-censor, 11-fore, 12-slough, 13-peddle, 14-away, 15-pedal, 16-toe, 17-revue, 18-petal, 19-bear, 20-review, 21-duel, 22-for.

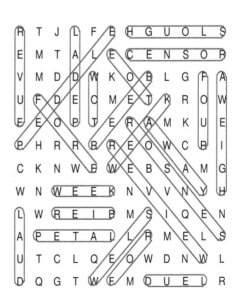

Homonyms 191-200, Puzzle 1

ACROSS: 5-might, 7-aye, 8-rigor, 9-rigueur, 11-eye, 13-whether, 14-traitor, 17-rigger, 19-lyre, 20-bury.
DOWN: 1-pier, 2-liar, 3-sloe, 4-hour, 6-trader, 10-peer, 12-mite, 13-weather, 15-our, 16-berry, 18-slow.

Puzzle 2

1-hour, 2-whether, 3-peer, 4-slow, 5-liar, 6-rigger, 7-might, 8-bury, 9-eye, 10-mite, 11-pier, 12-rigor, 13-sloe, 14-trader, 15-lyre, 16-weather, 17-aye, 18-I, 19-berry, 20-traitor, 21-rigueur, 22-our.

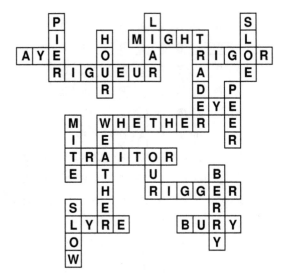

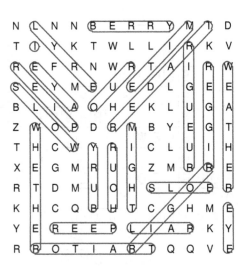

Puzzle 3

ACROSS: 2-slow, 4-bury, 5-rigger, 8-peer, 9-mite, 10-our, 11-traitor, 14-liar, 16-aye, 17-weather, 18-eye, 19-hour. DOWN: 1-lyre, 2-sloe, 3-whether, 4-berry, 6-rigueur, 7-rigor, 12-trader, 13-pier, 15-might.

Puzzle 4

1-whether, 2-peer, 3-hour, 4-might, 5-slow, 6-trader, 7-liar, 8-bury, 9-eye, 10-mite, 11-weather, 12-rigueur, 13-pier, 14-rigor, 15-sloe, 16-rigger, 17-traitor, 18-lyre, 19-aye, 20-I, 21-berry, 22-our.

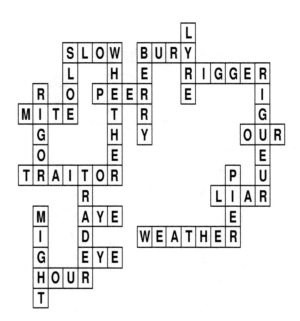

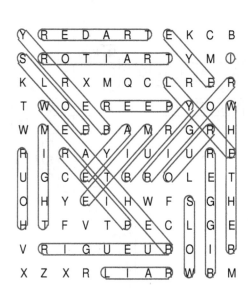

Homonyms 201-210, Puzzle 1

ACROSS: 2-missal, 5-which, 7-forward, 9-cent, 10-birth, 13-lie, 14-write, 16-missile, 18-right, 19-wright, 20-sent.
DOWN: 1-witch, 3-soar, 4-foreward, 6-humorous, 8-sore, 10-berth, 11-rite, 12-humerus, 13-lye, 15-pi, 17-pie.

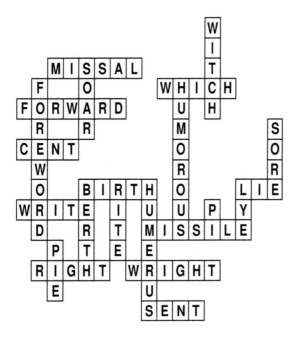

Puzzle 2

1-soar, 2-cent, 3-forward, 4-humorous, 5-pi, 6-right, 7-birth, 8-humerus, 9-rite, 10-lie, 11-which, 12-missile, 13-pie, 14-write, 15-sore, 16-witch, 17-lye, 18-berth, 19-sent, 20-missal, 21-wright, 22-foreward.

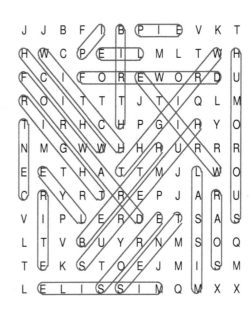

Puzzle 3

ACROSS: 2-missal, 4-wright, 5-foreward, 7-which, 9-rite, 12-lye, 13-humerus, 14-sore, 15-birth, 16-sent, 17-pi, 18-cent. DOWN: 1-pie, 3-soar, 4-write, 5-forward, 6-witch, 8-humorous, 9-right, 10-missile, 11-berth, 12-lie.

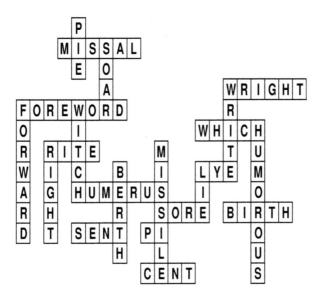

Puzzle 4

1-rite, 2-soar, 3-cent, 4-forward, 5-eight, 6-birth, 7-berth, 8-humerus, 9-lie, 10-humorous, 11-which, 12-wright, 13-missile, 14-write, 15-sore, 16-witch, 17-pie, 18-lye, 19-pi, 20-sent, 21-missal, 22-foreward.

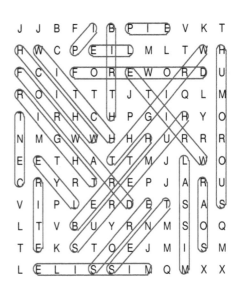

Homonyms 211-220, Puzzle 1

ACROSS: 2-fourth, 3-wile, 6-mote, 7-links, 10-bettor, 11-picture, 14-cents, 16-chili, 17-ring, 18-lynx, 19-sense.
DOWN: 1-soul, 3-while, 4-sole, 5-moat, 8-since, 9-forth, 10-better, 11-pitcher, 12-Chile, 13-wring, 14-chilly, 15-scents.

Puzzle 2

1-scents, 2-lynx, 3-chilly, 4-while, 5-since, 6-fourth, 7-links, 8-sole, 9-mote, 10-picture, 11-cents, 12-forth, 13-ring, 14-Chile, 15-wring, 16-soul, 17-wile, 18-better, 19-moat, 20-bettor, 21-sense, 22-pitcher, 23-chili.

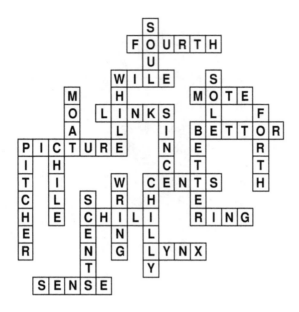

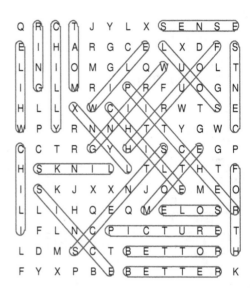

Puzzle 3

ACROSS: 2-sole, 5-chilly, 6-pitcher, 8-lynx, 9-since, 12-Chile, 15-bettor, 16-soul, 18-wring, 19-pitcher, 20-ring, 21-forth, 22-scents. DOWN: 1-moat, 3-while, 4-sense, 7-chili, 10-cents, 11-better, 13-fourth, 14-mote, 17-links, 18-wile.

Puzzle 4

1-scents, 2-chilly, 3-while, 4-picture, 5-wring, 6-since, 7-fourth, 8-pitcher, 9-bettor, 10-links, 11-sole, 12-mote, 13-cents, 14-forth, 15-Chile, 16-soul, 17-wile, 18-ring, 19-better, 20-moat, 21-lynx, 22-sense, 23-chili.

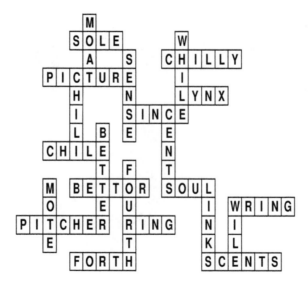

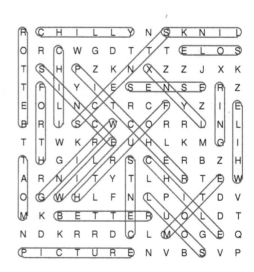

Homonyms 221-230, Puzzle 1

ACROSS: 1-foul, 4-mode, 5-fowl, 8-build, 10-some,
11-plane, 13-mowed, 15-billed, 17-rode, 18-plain.
DOWN: 2-lode, 3-rowed, 6-wine, 7-chute, 9-lone,
10-sum, 12-load, 14-whine, 16-loan, 17-road.

Puzzle 2

1-sum, 2-fowl, 3-load, 4-build, 5-road, 6-shoot,
7-mode, 8-plain, 9-whine, 10-plane, 11-rode,
12-some, 13-lode, 14-foul, 15-wine, 16-billed,
17-chute, 18-loan, 19-mowed, 20-lone, 21-rowed.

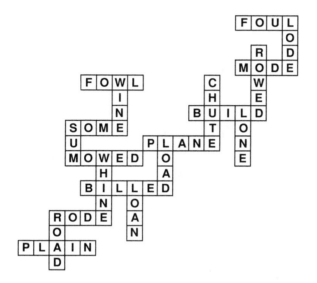

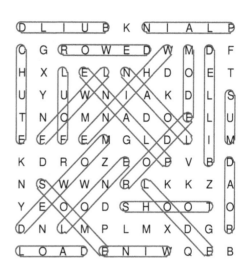

Puzzle 3

ACROSS: 3-shoot, 4-road, 6-foul, 7-whine, 9-load,
11-billed, 13-mode, 14-rode, 15-plane, 16-loan.
DOWN: 1-chute, 2-mowed, 4-rowed, 5-build, 6-fowl,
8-wine, 10-some, 12-lode, 15-plain, 16-lone.

Puzzle 4

1-sum, 2-road, 3-load, 4-fowl, 5-build, 6-shoot,
7-wine, 8-mode, 9-plain, 10-whine, 11-plane,
12-rode, 13-some, 14-foul, 15-rowed, 16-billed,
17-chute, 18-loan, 19-mowed, 20-lone, 21-lode.

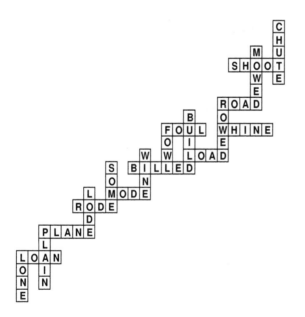

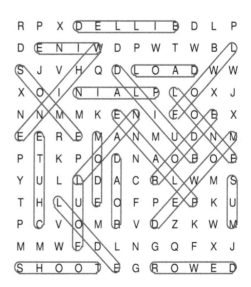

Homonyms 231-240, Puzzle 1

ACROSS: 3-lower, 9-whirled, 10-roe, 13-lore, 14-morning, 15-site, 17-mussel, 19-bite, 20-sum, 21-muscle. DOWN: 1-byte, 2-world, 4-row, 5-mourning, 6-please, 7-cite, 8-plumb, 11-pleas, 12-sight, 16-plumb, 18-son.

Puzzle 2

1-pleas, 2-mourning, 3-roe, 4-sight, 5-son, 6-lore, 7-bite, 8-whirled, 9-sum, 10-site, 11-world, 12-byte, 13-mussel, 14-cite, 15-row, 16-lower, 17-muscle, 18-please, 19-plum, 20-morning, 21-plumb.

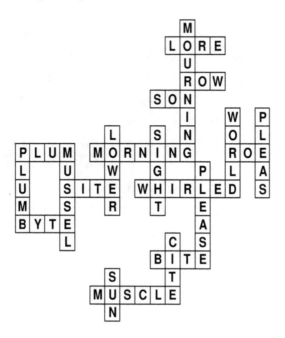

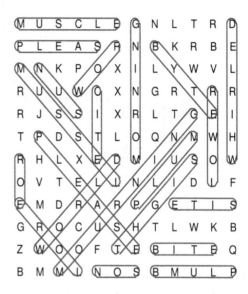

Puzzle 3

ACROSS: 2-lore, 3-row, 4-son, 9-plum, 11-morning, 12-roe, 14-site, 15-whirled, 16-byte, 18-bite, 20-muscle. DOWN: 1-mourning, 5-world, 6-pleas, 7-lower, 8-sight, 9-plumb, 10-mussel, 13-please, 17-cite, 19-sum.

Puzzle 4

1-site, 2-mourning, 3-roe, 4-lower, 5-son, 6-lore, 7-bite, 8-whirled, 9-sun, 10-sight, 11-world, 12-byte, 13-plum, 14-cite, 15-row, 16-pleas, 17-muscle, 18-please, 19-mussel, 20-morning, 21-plumb.

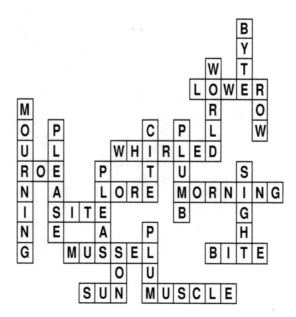

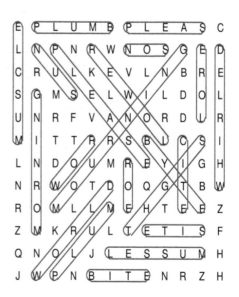

Homonyms 241-250, Puzzle 1

ACROSS: 1-mustard, 3-women, 7-roll, 8-blew, 10-pole 11-poll, 12-role, 13-clause, 14-wood, 15-sough, 16-sought. DOWN: 2-roil, 4-mustered, 5-sue, 6-royal, 8-blue, 9-woman, 13-claws, 14-would, 15-sot.

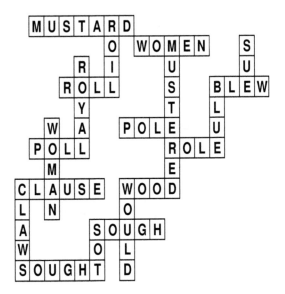

Puzzle 2

1-roil, 2-sot, 3-poll, 4-woman, 5-roll, 6-blew, 7-blue, 8-claws, 9-mustard, 10-women, 11-pole, 12-sought, 13-role, 14-sough, 15-royal, 16-wood, 17-mustered, 18-sue, 19-would, 20-clause.

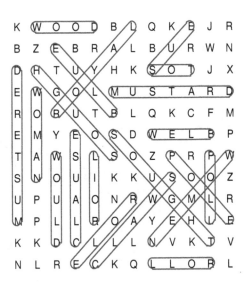

Puzzle 3

ACROSS: 4-poll, 5-would, 6-blue, 7-sue, 8-woman, 12-clause, 14-sought, 15-pole, 16-royal, 17-role, 18-wood. DOWN: 1-women, 2-sot, 3-claws, 6-blew, 9-mustered, 10-sough, 11-mustard, 13-roil, 17-roll.

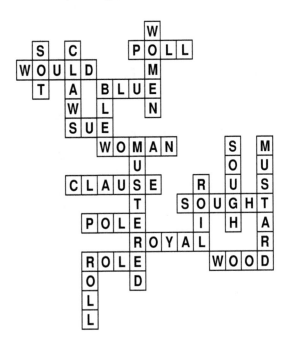

Puzzle 4

1-roil, 2-woman, 3-sought, 4-roll, 5-blew, 6-sue, 7-blue, 8-poll, 9-mustard, 10-women, 11-pole, 12-role, 13-sough, 14-royal, 15-sot, 16-wood, 17-mustered, 18-would, 19-claws, 20-clause.

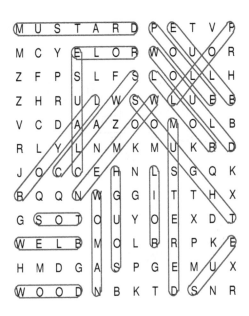

224

Homonyms 251-260, Puzzle 1

ACROSS: 2-rote, 4-pour, 5-cord, 7-bore, 9-chord, 11-compliment, 13-staph, 17-praise, 18-stare, 19-boar, 20-staff, 21-wrote. DOWN: complement, 3-board, 6-root, 8-bored, 10-route, 12-preys, 14-prays, 15-stair, 16-poor, 17-pore.

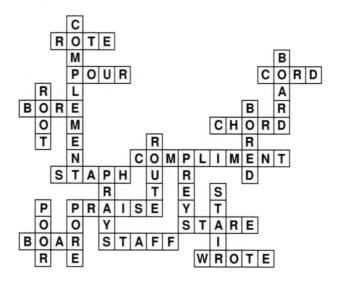

Puzzle 2

1-boar, 2-pore, 3-staff, 4-stare, 5-compliment, 6-cord, 7-pour, 8-route, 9-stair, 10-board, 11-complement, 12-chord, 13-praise, 14-poor, 15-bored, 16-preys, 17-memory, 18-wrote, 19-bore, 20-prays, 21-staph, 22-root.

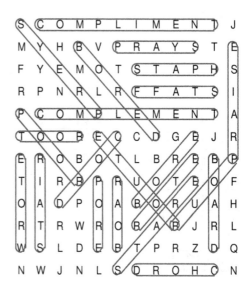

Puzzle 3

ACROSS: 4-pore, 6-chord, 9-route, 10-stare, 11-poor, 12-staph, 13-praise, 17-compliment, 19-boar, 20-root, 21-staff. DOWN: 1-bore, 2-bored, 3-prays, 5-pour, 6-cord, 7-complement, 8-wrote, 14-rote, 15-stair, 16-board, 18-preys.

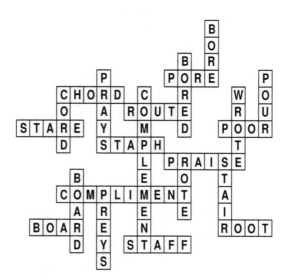

Puzzle 4

1-preys, 2-boar, 3-route, 4-pore, 5-staff, 6-rote, 7-compliment, 8-praise, 9-cord, 10-pour, 11-stair, 12-bored, 13-complement, 14-chord, 15-poor, 16-stare, 17-bored, 18-wrote, 19-bore, 20-staph, 21-root, 22-prays.

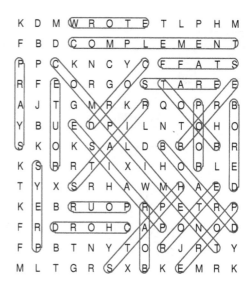

Homonyms 261-270, Puzzle 1

ACROSS: 1-counsel, 2-border, 4-rough, 6-stalk, -stock, 8-principle, 11-rout, 12-bode, 14-steal, 15-council, 16-presence. DOWN: 1-counselor, 2-boarder, 3-ruff, 5-councilor, 8-presents, 9-principal, 10-bowed, 13-route, 14-steel.

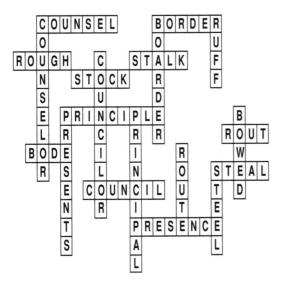

Puzzle 2

1-rough, 2-border, 3-council, 4-stock, 5-route, 6-principal, 7-presents, 8-counselor, 9-steal, 10-principle, 11-ruff, 12-stalk, 13-bode, 14-bowed, 15-counsel, 16-boarder, 17-steel, 18-councilor, 19-presence, 20-rout.

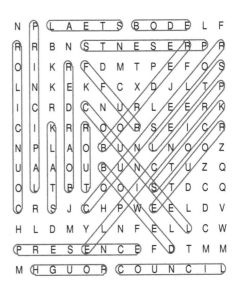

Puzzle 3

ACROSS: 3-councilor, 8-principal, 9-counsel, 12-counselor, 13-bode, 14-presents, 17-route, 18-rough, 19-steal. DOWN: 1-ruff, 2-council, 4-steal, 5-principle, 6-stock, 7-presence, 10-bowed, 11-boarder, 13-border, 15-stalk, 16-rout.

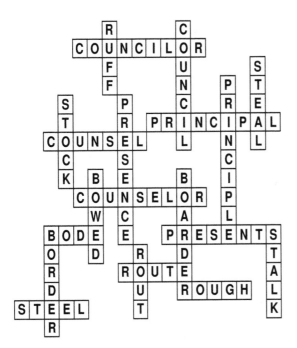

Puzzle 4

1-rough, 2-presents, 3-council, 4-stock, 5-route, 6-principal, 7-counsel, 8-steal, 9-principle, 10-presence, 11-border, 12-ruff, 13-bode, 14-bowed, 15-boarder, 16-counselor, 17-stalk, 18-steel, 19-councilor, 20-rout.

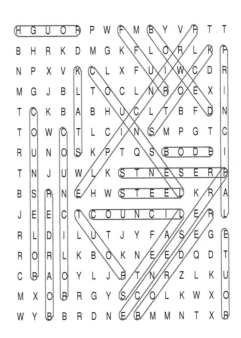

Homonyms 271-280, Puzzle 1

ACROSS: 2-breaches, 4-burro, 5-born, 6-strait, 8-bow, 9-breeches, 12-straight, 13-rung, 15-creek, 16-wrung. DOWN: 1-creak, 2-burrow, 3-stile, 4-borne, 5-break, 7-prose, 8-bough, 9-borough, 10-style, 11-brake, 14-pros.

Puzzle 2

1-borne, 2-creak, 3-prose, 4-bough, 5-brake, 6-breaches, 7-rung, 8-style, 9-borough, 10-burro, 11-pros, 12-straight, 13-born, 14-bow, 15-burrow, 16-strait, 17-stile, 18-break, 19-creak, 20-breeches, 21-wrung.

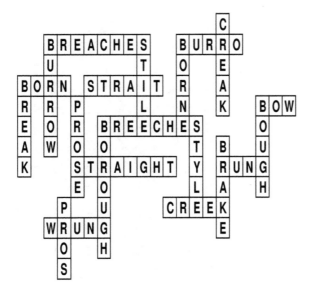

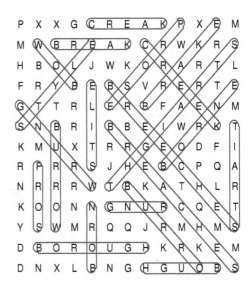

Puzzle 3

ACROSS: 2-born, 4-burro, 5-bow, 6-style, 7-break, 10-breaches, 12-borne, 16-straight, 17-creak. DOWN: 1-rung, 2-borough, 3-prose, 4-breeches, 5-brake, 8-wrung, 9-burrow, 11-strait, 12-bough, 13-pros, 14-stile, 15-creek.

Puzzle 4

1-borne, 2-straight, 3-prose, 4-bough, 5-brake, 6-breaches, 7-bow, 8-creek, 9-style, 10-borough, 11-burro, 12-pros, 13-born, 14-burrow, 15-strait, 16-rung, 17-creak, 18-stile, 19-break, 20-breeches, 21-wrung.

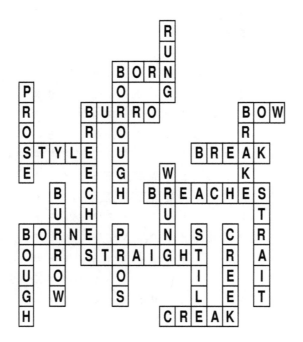

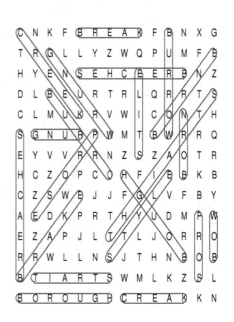

Homonyms 281-290, Puzzle 1
ACROSS: 1-bye, 2-by, 3-corps, 5-whoa, 8-coup,
9-sweet, 11-bridle, 12-Finnish, 14-core, 15-bread, 16-coo,
17-serge. DOWN: 1-buy, 2-bridal, 4-sweat, 6-coupe,
7-woe, 9-suite, 10-finish, 11-bred, 13-surge, 14-coop.

Puzzle 2
1-buy, 2-sweat, 3-bread, 4-coup, 5-finish, 6-coop,
7-bridal, 8-bye, 9-coo, 10-core, 11-Finnish,
12-surge, 13-bred, 14-whoa, 15-bridle, 16-coupe,
17-serge, 18-corps, 19-suite, 20-woe, 21-sweet,
22-by.

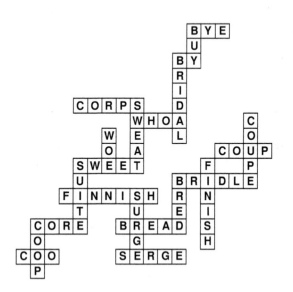

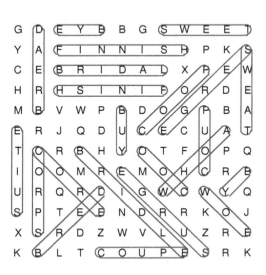

Puzzle 3
ACROSS: 1-bye, 2-buy, 4-finish, 6-whoa, 7-bread,
8-coo, 9-sweat, 10-coupe, 11-core, 12-sweet, 14-bridle,
15-Finnish. DOWN: 1-by, 2-bridal, 3-bred, 5-serge,
6-woe, 8-coup, 9-surge, 10-coop, 12-suite, 13-corps.

Puzzle 4
1-buy, 2-sweat, 3-bye, 4-coup, 5-finish, 6-coop,
7-corps, 8-suite, 9-woe, 10-sweet, 11-bridal,
12-coo, 13-core, 14-Finnish, 15-surge, 16-bred,
17-whoa, 18-bridle, 19-bread, 20-coupe, 21-serge,
22-by.

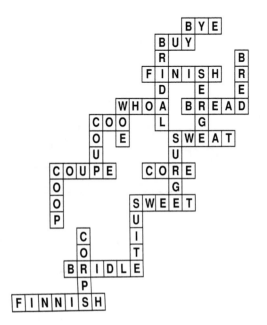

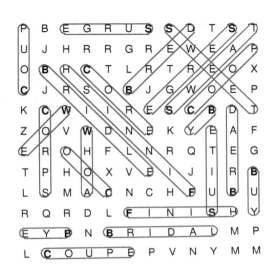

Order Form

Thank you for using *Spelling Made Easy*. We hope you've enjoyed it. Everyday Education offers a number of other high school and middle school resources that you might find helpful. Please visit the website at www.Everyday-Education for complete information about each product and to place your order.

If you prefer to order offline, please send the form below, along with your check, money order, or credit card information to: Everyday Education, LLC, 13041 Hill Club Lane, Ashland, VA 23005-3150. We ship via Priority Mail.

Quantity	Item	Each	Total
	Resources for Middle School and High School		
	Grammar Made Easy: Writing a Step Above	29.00	
	Grammar Made Easy with Extended Keys	39.00	
	Transcripts Made Easy: The Homeschooler's Guide to High School Paperwork	24.95	
	Get a Jump Start on College: A Practical Guide for Teens	18.00	
	Evaluate Writing the Easy Way	7.95	
	Excellence in Literature: Reading and Writing Through the Classics (Grades 8-12)		
	English I: Introduction to Literature	29.00	
	English II: Literature and Composition	29.00	
	English III: American Literature	29.00	
	English IV: British Literature	29.00	
	English V: World Literature	29.00	
	Subtotal		
	Tax (5% for VA residents only)		
	Shipping ($4.95 for 1-2 items; $9.90 for 3 or more)		
	Order total		

Ship To:

Name _____

Address _____

City, State, Zip _____

E-mail address _____